In The Sanctuary

In The Sanctuary

Expository Sermons on
the Lord's Prayer

BY

HERMAN HOEKSEMA

REFORMED FREE PUBLISHING ASSOCIATION
Grand Rapids, Michigan

Library of Congress Card Number:
81-84057

ISBN 0-916206-25-4

PRINTED IN THE UNITED STATES OF AMERICA

EDITOR'S PREFACE

This little volume, first published in 1943, was originally a series of radio messages on the important subject of prayer based on that perfect model which the Lord Jesus Himself left us. In the preface to the original version of this book the author himself stated, "Perhaps, if I had had the time to revise them, I would have improved the form, though I feel that the contents would have remained unaltered." The author lacked that time for revision, and so these messages were originally published in the very form in which they were prepared for broadcasting. We have tried to polish the form somewhat and to eliminate those aspects of these chapters peculiar to their broadcast-form.

We add the same wish as did the author in the original volume: "May God so bless this publication that it may be a means to impress upon us more deeply that God is GOD, and that we should be conscious of this fundamental truth in our prayer, so that we may learn and earnestly endeavor to pray in harmony with the will of God, and in that way experience that He always hears us."

— Homer C. Hoeksema

CONTENTS

Chapter 1

TRUE PRAYER

As we introduce the subject of prayer, we may well impress upon your mind that it is a very difficult subject to treat. This is true, first of all, because of the very nature of the subject itself. Prayer is a holy art; and if we would analyze it and expound some of its underlying principles, we will have to approach our task in an attitude of holy reverence. It is the highest possible expression of what lives in the believer's heart by grace. Not in our works, not in our sacrifices and offerings, but in our speech, in the word of our mouth, and particularly in our prayers it is that God is glorified the most. Because prayer is an art, a holy art, the Christian will have to become truly efficient in prayer by practice and experience.

This does not mean, however, that there are no underlying principles which control this holy art of prayer and which must be observed by those who are occupied with it. These principles can be derived only from the Word of God itself. We must allow ourselves to be instructed by Scripture in order to bring into practice more consciously and fully the underlying principles of true prayer, that thus we may become more efficient in this holy, spiritual art. In the light of Scripture we must answer such questions as: What is prayer? To whom do we pray? For what may we pray? What is the proper attitude of prayer?

But difficult this subject is, too, because there is, perhaps, no subject on which there is so much misunderstanding as on the subject of prayer. How often is prayer, which properly is the chief medium for the glorification of God, considered a means to obtain the fulfillment of our own carnal desires! How often, while it should be the most humble expression of submission to the will of the Father in heaven, it appears to be an attempt to impose our will upon the Almighty! And how frequently, while prayer is properly the seeking of the things of the kingdom of God and His righteousness, it is nothing but the expression of earthly desires! The reason is that we are still largely carnal, and that carnal and earthly things often weigh more heavily with us than things that are spiritual and heavenly. It is expedient, therefore, that we always compare our own prayers with that most perfect prayer which the Lord taught us to pray; and in this discussion of prayer we will do well to follow its lead.

There are innumerable passages in Holy Writ that speak of prayer, both in the Old and in the New Testament. Throughout Scripture we find that the people of God are a praying people, even from earliest times. Without prayer they cannot live. It is the very breath of their spiritual life. They cry to Jehovah in their distress, they call upon His name in the day of trouble, they seek His grace and fellowship, they worship and adore Him, they praise Him and give Him thanks. Almost all the psalms assume the form of prayer and praise. Besides, many other prayers of eminent saints are preserved for us in the Bible, such as the prayers of Abraham and Moses, of David and Solomon, of Isaiah and Hezekiah, of Daniel and Nehemiah, of Elijah and of the remnant according to the election of grace, of the church in Jerusalem and of Paul. Surpassing them all, both in spiritual beauty and perfection of contents, we have the prayers of the Lord Jesus: His marvelous sacerdotal prayer as recorded in John 17, and that profound expression of perfect submission to the will of the Father which He uttered in the hour of His agony in Gethsemane. Our Lord once spake a parable to teach us that we should always pray and never faint, even though God is longsuffering over His people. (Luke 18:1-8) In the sermon on the mount, He assures us: "Ask, and it shall be given you; seek, and ye shall find; knock, and it shall be opened unto you: For every one that asketh receiveth; and he that seeketh findeth; and to him that knocketh it shall be opened." (Matthew 7:7, 8) We are admonished to continue instant in prayer (Romans 12:12), and to pray without ceasing. (I Thessalonians 5:17) And, "The effectual fervent prayer of a righteous man availeth much." (James 5:16) The Lord Jesus left us a model prayer which, though not intended to be copied literally only, is a concrete illustration of all the principles that should underlie our prayers.

There are, of course, different forms of prayer and different occasions for prayer. Scripture employs different terms to express different aspects of this holy engagement of the whole soul. In the Old Testament a word is used which denotes the act of exhibiting or exposing one's cause before the Lord. Another term has the same root in it as the word for *grace* and is often translated by our word *supplication.* It denotes the act of invoking God's favor, grace, pity, or mercy. Still another word, translated by "cry," is used to denote the prayer of him who is in distress or tribulation and who cries to Jehovah for help and deliverance. Also in the New Testament we find several words for prayer. There is the word which is translated by our English term *worship,* which vividly expresses the proper attitude of him who presents himself before the face of the Most High, the attitude of deep humility and profound reverence. Other terms emphasize such ideas as confidence, fellowship with God, or devotion to the Most High. The activity of prayer as such is also variously expressed in Scripture. Prayer is called a lifting up of one's soul to God, a calling upon the name of the Lord, a seeking of Him or of His face, a bowing toward His holy place, an entering into His sanctuary, a drawing near unto the Lord, a crying unto Him from the depths, a pouring out of one's heart before Him, a waiting patiently for Him, and even a thirsting and panting of the soul after Him.

Considering all these different Scriptural data, we may conclude that all true prayer contains the following elements:
1) It is a holy activity of the entire soul, proceeding from the regenerated heart, dominated by the Spirit of Christ.
2) It is such an activity of the believer as brings him consciously into the presence of God in the face of Christ Jesus, so that he presents himself before His face.
3) Hence, all true prayer is always an act of worship whereby the soul prostrates itself before the glory of God's infinite majesty in humble reverence.

4) It is the expression of a real sense of need, principally of God and of His grace, and of a profound longing for Him and His fellowship, and of the heartfelt desire that He hear us and fulfill our need.

5) Finally, true prayer is the assurance and confidence that He will receive us and give unto us that which we ask of Him, rooted in the consciousness of His great love to usward.

Briefly, prayer is the activity of the believer whereby he acknowledges the living God as the sole and overflowing fountain of all good and approaches that fountain with the earnest desire to drink from its blessed water of life.

In all true prayer, then, we address the true and living God. You may, perhaps, think that this is a mere platitude; but if it is, it surely can bear repeating and emphasis. But what does it mean that we direct our prayer to the living God? It means nothing less than that in our prayers we are wholly dominated and guided by the true knowledge of God in the face of Christ Jesus our Lord, as He has revealed Himself in His Word. This is paramount. Only thus is it possible for us to place ourselves in the presence of the God of our salvation, to enter into His holy place, to present ourselves before His face, to worship Him and to have communion with Him. I must know Him, the only true God, in order to be able to pray at all. But I cannot know Him out of myself, I cannot find Him out. Whatever *I* say about God is sure to be a lie; whatever god of my own imagination I may attempt to make is sure to be an idol. Only He can make known to me Who He is, and what He is. Hence, I must let Him speak to me before I can even begin to speak to Him. This He does in His Word, in the Holy Scriptures. For though it is true that the invisible things of Him are also clearly discerned from the things that are made, yet I cannot know Him as the God of my salvation, Who forgives iniquities, and to Whom I can pray, except from His own Word revealed in Christ Jesus our Lord, contained in the Holy Scriptures. The conclusion from this is evident: the more fully and thoroughly God's people are instructed in the true knowledge of God, the more efficient they will become in the holy, spiritual art of prayer.

From this one fundamental truth follows all we will have to say about prayer in the rest of this chapter.

For, first of all, the consciousness that in our prayers we are addressing the true and living God must needs determine the contents of our prayer. It means that we will not pray thoughtlessly, asking for anything that may come into our minds. But that we will pray with holy intelligence, instructed as to the contents of our petitions by His Word and Spirit. It implies that we are consciously speaking to that great God, Who made all things for His own name's sake, so that in our prayers we are not seeking our own little carnal end, but God Himself, His name, His kingdom, His glory, His cause, and His will. It signifies that we are consciously addressing the absolute Sovereign of heaven and earth, Who governs all things according to His eternal good pleasure, and Whose counsel shall stand forever. And this means that He is omniscient, so that we do not have to inform Him about conditions in the world; for He knows what we need, far better than we do, before we ask Him.

It means, too, that He is the all-wise God, Who governs all things with perfect wisdom, and Who never fails in His judgment, so that in our prayers we do not attempt to inform Him of our judgment as to the way He ought to govern our lives and all things in the world, but we rather humbly beseech Him for grace to submit our judgment to His, and ask Him to show us His way, that we may walk therein. It means also that our prayers are not an attempt to impose our will upon the will of the Almighty, but rather a humble petition for grace that we may submit our will to His and may learn to will His will. For "this is the confidence that we have in him, that, if we ask anything according to his will, he heareth us." (I John 5:14) Frequently the question is asked: does prayer change things? It is very popular to answer this question in the affirmative. I can agree with this, provided you mean that it pleases God to execute His own unchangeable counsel and to cause His own kingdom to come in the way of the prayers of His saints, prayers which He Himself works in their hearts by His Spirit and instructs them to pray by His Word. But if you should mean that by our prayers we change the will and mind of the absolute Sovereign of all the universe, so that through our prayers not His will, but our will is done, I make bold to state not only that I must utterly disagree with such a view of prayer, but also that I abhor it with all my soul. If ever I felt as if by my prayer I changed the mind of the ever-living God, never would I have the courage to utter another petition! We do not approach the overflowing fount of all good in order to pour anything of ourselves into it and add to its sparkling goodness, but with the empty cups of our existence, that they may be filled by Him!

But still more follows from this one principle that in our prayers we consciously address the living God as He has revealed Himself in His Word. In this consciousness the sense of our real need is quite different from what we usually, in our earthly-mindedness and carnality, conceive it to be. For, as we present ourselves before the face of the living God, we are impressed and overwhelmed with a sense of His holiness. And in that sense many of our imagined needs begin to appear as the product of our sinful desires. Perhaps we had in our heart to pray for prosperity, for meat and drink, for abundance of earthly things, for health and joy, for peace and earthly happiness for ourselves and our children. But as we really stand face to face with the Holy One of Israel, we deeply realize that all these desires are carnal and sinful, that they represent the things after which the Gentiles seek, and our intended petitions die on our lips. Perhaps there is sickness in our home, and we are not satisfied with God's way. We approach the throne of grace, firmly determined to beseech the Lord of all to remove the sickness and to restore to health. But as we stand in the presence of the Most High, we realize that He knows better than we what we really need, and that He sends us all things in order to prepare us for His eternal kingdom. Then we change our prayer into a petition for grace to will His will. Perhaps we thought, as Asaph, that we had reason to murmur and to criticize the ways of the Almighty because we see the wicked prosper, while our punishment is there every morning. But in the sanctuary of God we see all things in the light of the end; and, shamefaced because of our murmuring spirit, we now confess that it is good for us to be near unto God. Perhaps there is war in the world, destruction and madness, devastation and death; and our sons are called to battle. Quite thoughtlessly, even considering it an act of piety, we hastened to the throne of the Almighty and earnestly meant to beseech Him to stop the war at once and to restore peace. But as soon as we are really and consciously in the presence of His majesty, we hear Him say: "I, the Lord, am He that doeth all these things. I make peace, but I also cause war to come. And all these things are subservient to the realization of My counsel and the coming of My kingdom." And with fear and trembling we choke back our intended petition for peace and say, "Thy will be done!" Oh, it is easy in our prayers to ask the questions of anxiety and earthly-mindedness, "What shall we eat?" and, "What shall we drink?" and, "Wherewithall shall we be clothed?" as long as we really pray to an idol. But as soon as prayers become petitions to the living and only true God, all these carnal petitions die on our lips and we begin to seek first the kingdom of God and His righteousness, confident that all other things shall be added unto us.

This one principle also determines the spiritual attitude which we assume in our prayers. Concerning this, I may mention especially three elements that are paramount: true humility, truth in our inmost heart, and childlike confidence.

Humility will characterize our attitude in prayer if we approach Him in the consciousness of His glory and majesty. This means, first of all, that we know that He is the Lord, the fulness of all riches, the overflowing fountain of all good, and that we are empty, always in need of Him. We can never bring anything to Him, or add anything to His infinite fulness. We come then with our little empty cups to the fountain, that they may be filled. God is all, we are nothing! That is true humility. But it implies more. For we are sinners, and we have forfeited all things. True humility, therefore, also means that we approach Him with the confession of our utter unworthiness in ourselves to receive ought from Him, yea, of our worthiness of being damned. And thus, this true humility will make us realize that we can approach Him only in Christ Jesus and on the ground of His perfect righteousness, and that we are, above all, in need of grace.

But the knowledge that we present ourselves before the living God, "Who knows all our hearts, and the secrets within," will also impress upon us that we must come before Him with truth in the inmost

heart. We cannot approach Him with a lie in our right hand. We must
feel in our hearts that we really desire the things we ask of Him. We
must really hunger and thirst after righteousness when we ask Him for
the forgiveness of sins and for the deliverance from evil. We must really
have forgiven one another before we can appear before Him with the
prayer "Forgive us our debts, as we forgive our debtors." We must
really desire that His name be glorified, that His kingdom may come,
that His will may be done, and that, too, regardless of what may
become of our name, of our kingdom, of our will, in order to utter
before Him the first three petitions of the Lord's Prayer. For He
requires truth in our inmost hearts.

Thus, finally, we will also approach Him in the attitude of confidence that He will grant us our petition. For He that cometh unto
God must believe that He is, and that He is a rewarder of them that
diligently seek Him. (Hebrews 11:6) We shall be able to close our
prayers with a real and true *Amen,* confident, not merely that He
shall give us *something* but that He shall grant us exactly what we asked
of Him according to His will. And the blessed fruit for us will be that
He will abundantly give us His grace and Spirit, and that "the peace
of God, which passeth all understanding, shall keep your hearts and
minds through Christ Jesus." (Philippians 4:7)

Chapter 2

THE PRINCIPLES OF THE LORD'S PRAYER

"After this manner therefore pray ye: Our Father which art in heaven, Hallowed be thy name. Thy kingdom come. Thy will be done in earth, as it is in heaven. Give us this day our daily bread. And forgive us our debts, as we forgive our debtors. And lead us not into temptation, but deliver us from evil: For thine is the kingdom, and the power, and the glory, for ever. Amen." (Matthew 6:9-13)

Thus the Lord taught us to pray.

Before we enter into a detailed discussion of this most perfect prayer, before we set our feet across the threshold of this holy of holies, and dwell for a moment in every hall and chamber of this sanctuary, we will do well to examine the grandeur and beauty and perfection of the whole. For it is not only from the separate petitions of this model prayer that the Lord Jesus would have His people learn how they should pray; but He also would teach us some of the most fundamental underlying principles of true prayer by the order of the various petitions and by the relation in which they stand to one another. "After this manner therefore pray ye." This does not mean that in the Lord's Prayer we have a fixed form from which we never dare to part in our own prayers; but it certainly signifies that this prayer is a model the main lines of which we must always copy, and the chief principles of which we may never violate when we approach the throne of grace with our petitions. In order to discover these, we must not be too hasty to analyze the Lord's Prayer and to expound its details, but we must rather tarry awhile to contemplate the beauty and meaning of its style.

We notice at once that this prayer is characterized by simple brevity,

17

on the one hand, yet by fulness and completeness, on the other hand. In the immediate context the Lord had taught His disciples that they should not use "vain repetitions, as the heathen do: for they think that they shall be heard for their much speaking. Be not ye therefore like unto them: for your Father knoweth what things ye have need of, before ye ask him." (Matthew 6:7, 8) This principle is certainly embodied in the Lord's Prayer. It is so brief and simple that it requires no more than half a minute to recite it, and a small child can easily learn it by heart. This does not mean that we may not dwell in this holy place of prayer much longer than the time required to recite this prayer. Nor does it imply that we may never employ more words in our prayers. The contrary is true. It is well for us, who are often so occupied with earthly matters that it is difficult for us to enter into the sanctuary and to lift up our hearts to the Holy One, that we take much time to separate ourselves unto prayer. And when we really pour out our hearts in prayer, we may well have need of many more words than we find in the Lord's Prayer to worship and adore and glorify the Most High and to drink from the fountain of life and all good. But it does mean that we must never assume the attitude of one who presumes to inform God about mundane matters, nor the attitude of the headstrong child who seeks to obtain what he wants by his importunity. Your Father knows what you need before you ask Him. Hence, you need not employ vain repetitions in order to explain your needs to Him. Neither do you have to persuade Him to fulfill your real needs. But while the Lord's Prayer is very brief, it is not lacking in contents on that account. On the contrary, it is a perfect whole. It contains a fulness of petitions. The Christian cannot think of anything more to ask than that which is expressed in this model prayer. Whatever he prays in addition to the contents of the Lord's Prayer, or contrary to it, is certainly not according to the will of God. The marvel of this prayer, then, is that while it is so extremely simple and brief, it fully expresses all that the Christian in this world needs.

These principles of all true prayer cannot be emphasized too much, especially in view of the fact that there is so much misunderstanding and corruption of this holiest of arts. If one listens to many prayers and to many statements about prayer, one cannot but receive the impression that this spiritual exercise is looked upon as merely a means to obtain from the Lord what we want. We can pray for anything we desire, it seems; and if only we press our urgent requests and pray with sufficient pertinacity, the Lord will be persuaded by us and will grant our requests. We are heard because of our much speaking. Our prayers do change the mind of God, or, at least, His ways with us. An appeal is made to Scripture to substantiate this conception of prayer.

Permit me to call your attention to one of the several passages of the Word of God that are quoted in support of what I nevertheless must consider a very corrupt and carnal conception of prayer, a passage that is perhaps more often appealed to than any other. I am referring to the prayer of Hezekiah, the king of Judah. You are all acquainted, no doubt, with the incident in Hezekiah's life which occasioned the prayer, as well as with the prayer itself and its result. The king was sick, and his sickness was fatal. Moreover, the Word of the Lord came unto him by the mouth of the prophet Isaiah: "Set thine house in order; for thou shalt die, and not live." (II Kings 20:1) But Hezekiah was not ready to set his house in order and to die, and he prayed earnestly to the Lord: "I beseech thee, O Lord, remember now how I have walked before thee in truth and with a perfect heart, and have done that which is good in thy sight." (vs. 3) In answer to that prayer the prophet Isaiah was ordered to turn back to the king at once with this message: "Thus saith the Lord, the God of David thy father, I have heard thy prayer, I have seen thy tears: behold, I will heal thee: on the third day thou shalt go up unto the house of the Lord. And I will add unto thy days fifteen years; and I will deliver thee and this city out of the hand of the king of Assyria; and I will defend this city for mine own sake, and for my servant David's sake." (vss. 5, 6) And the king recovered from his fatal disease.

Now there are here especially two questions which are of interest and importance in connection with our present discussion of the subject of prayer. The first question is: did Hezekiah in this case not pray directly against the will of the Lord, and did he by his prayer not change the mind of the Most High and God's way with him? And does not this prayer, then, furnish us with a firm ground for the view that we also may do the same thing and expect the same results? Is it not a real proof of faith and piety, when we are sick, to turn in prayer to the Lord and beseech Him to heal us that we may not die? The second question, closely related to the first, is this: do we not have here a clear illustration and proof that the Lord does change His mind sometimes upon our request?

Both of these questions I must answer with a most emphatic *No!*

In ordinary circumstances we have no ground for the prayer that God may send recovery when we are sick, nor a promise of God that He will hear such a prayer. And if our sickness is of such a nature that through it the Lord says to us, "Prepare thy house, for thou shalt die, and not live," it is not pious to turn our face to the wall and weep, and let the Lord know that we are neither prepared nor willing to leave the earthly house of this tabernacle and to move to our heavenly house of God. In such cases we should answer: "Yes, Lord, I will be ready in a minute; it will not take me long to set my earthly house in order." I say: this applies to ordinary circumstances. But the circumstances under which Hezekiah prayed were quite extraordinary; in fact, they were such that he could plead on the basis of God's own sure promises against the word of the Lord that now came unto him, both through his sickness and by the mouth of Isaiah. What were these circumstances? They were first of all, that Jerusalem and Judah were threatened with destruction by the world power of Assyria. Evidently it was before Jerusalem had been delivered from the power of that mighty and ravening enemy that Hezekiah became sick and that he felt that he could not set his house in order and die. And we cannot fail to notice that the promise which he received upon his prayer for recovery includes the assurance that Jerusalem shall be delivered out of the hand of the king of Assyria. But this is not all. In the abstract, it was quite conceivable that Hezekiah should die and that the Lord would deliver the city through his successor on the throne. But it is evident from the text in its context that, when Hezekiah was stricken with this fatal disease, he had as yet no son. There was no seed of

David! And that made it absolutely impossible for the king to set his
house in order and die. It was exactly in this respect that he could
base his plea for recovery on the sure promise of God. Had not God
established His covenant with the house of David? He had! Definitely,
he had promised His servant David, according to II Samuel 7:12-16:
"I will set up thy seed after thee, which shall proceed out of thy
bowels, and I will establish his kingdom. He shall build an house for
my name, and I will establish the throne of his kingdom for ever. I
will be his father, and he shall be my son. If he commit iniquity, I
will chasten him with the rod of man, and with the stripes of the
children of men: but my mercy shall not depart from him, as I took it
from Saul, whom I put away before thee. And thine house and thy
kingdom shall be established for ever before thee: thy throne shall be
established for ever." On the basis of this promise Hezekiah could
plead for recovery, even against the Word of the Lord that was sent
to him at that moment. He could not possibly die, for he had no son.
Had he died at that time, the seed of David would have been cut off;
Christ would not have come!

It is true that the king does not literally mention this ground in his
prayer. But it is equally true that he does plead, not on the basis of
a certain self-righteousness, but on the ground of the fact that he had
walked in the way of that covenant of God when he says: "I beseech
thee, O Lord, remember now how I have walked before thee in truth
and with a perfect heart, and have done that which is good in thy
sight." There was no reason why God should take the covenant of
David away from him, as it had been removed from the house of Saul.
And it is equally true that in God's answer to Hezekiah's prayer this
ground of the Davidic covenant is plainly referred to. For Isaiah must
answer the king: "Thus saith the Lord, *the God of David thy father,*
I have seen thy tears: behold, I will heal thee." The conclusion, therefore, which you may draw from this incident of Hezekiah's prayer, is
not that when you are sick the Lord will surely heal you, if you only
pray persistently; but that the Lord will surely hear the prayer that is
based upon His own covenant and promise, no matter what may
be the circumstances.

This also answers, in part at least, the second question: did God in this particular instance change His mind? Of course not! He never had in mind to let Hezekiah die and to discontinue His covenant with David, ultimately with Christ. How could He, Who is faithful and true? What then? Did the Lord lie when He sent His Word to the king, "Thou shalt die, and not live"? God forbid that we should entertain such a thought even for a moment! He merely dealt with Hezekiah as He often deals with us and with all His children: pedagogically, for his instruction. To accomplish this He revealed His complete will to the king piecemeal, bit by bit, in order that he, and also Isaiah and the remnant according to the election of grace, might be tested, cry unto the Lord, and thus be purified and strengthened in their faith in Jehovah their God. For it was the Lord's full counsel in this case that He should test them by bringing the king to the edge of the grave, and to the certainty of death, in order that thus He might teach them to cry unto the Lord, and in the way of prayer might show them His mercy and deliver them. Often the Lord makes it dark and apparently hopeless for His cause and people in the world, in order that they may learn not to put their confidence in princes, but to cry to the Lord Sabaoth and to trust that salvation is of the Lord.

But let us now return to the Lord's Prayer and once more contemplate its perfection.

We may notice that the prayer presupposes a certain subject and a certain standpoint of that subject: the Christian as he stands in the midst of this present world. This prayer is frequently uttered in public gatherings and before mixed audiences in the world. There seems to be a notion that it is especially adapted for this purpose. But nothing could be farther from the truth. It is not the world of the ungodly, which cannot pray, nor mere man as such who is the subject of the Lord's Prayer; but it is very definitely the redeemed and regenerated and sanctified child of God. From the address of this prayer to its doxology, there is not a petition which fits in the mouth of the natural man, not even the prayer for daily bread. It is the believer who is able to address God as his Father in heaven, who is concerned about the name, and the kingdom, and the will of God, who is in need of the forgiveness of sins, and who longs for the deliverance from evil. It is the Christian who truly acknowledges that God's only is the kingdom, and the power, and the glory for ever. But it is the Christian as he is in this world. In heaven, in the new creation wherein righteousness shall dwell, we shall also pray, of course. But we shall then be able to pray the Lord's Prayer no longer. Then God's name shall forever be hallowed in perfection: for His kingdom shall have come, and therefore His will shall be done in earth and heaven. Then we shall no longer need bread, and we shall not be in daily need of forgiveness; nor shall there be any more evil or danger of temptation. It is in this world only that we need bread, and that we need it for just one day, no more. And it is in this world, too, that we need the grace of forgiveness and of deliverance from the evil one. The standpoint of him who utters this prayer, therefore, is that of the believer in the present world and state of imperfection and battle. Let no one deceive himself into imagining that this prayer is especially adapted to be prayed in public gatherings of mixed audiences. On the other hand, let no one assume the position that it requires ultimate perfection to pray after the manner of the Lord's Prayer.

Let us now look somewhat more closely at the structure and composition of this perfect model of prayer, at the number and order of the separate petitions contained in it. We notice that the prayer consists of three main parts: the address, or allocution, the various petitions, and the close, or doxology. The meaning and contents of these several parts we expect to discuss in later chapters. At present, however, we must examine especially the order of the different petitions.

It strikes us immediately that these petitions may be divided into two groups, and that the first of these groups is concerned wholly and exclusively with God and with His cause in the world, while the second group has reference to our needs. The first group contains three petitions; and if we may distinguish four petitions in the second group, which is not impossible, we find the number of God Triune, and the number of the world, or of the creature, represented here. Together these symbolize the perfection of God's kingdom and covenant by the number seven. Be this as it may, there is a very definite principle clearly taught in the order of the two groups, namely, that in our prayer we are concerned with God above all and in the first place, and with ourselves only in the second place, and for His sake. Now this is a very important, yea, even the all-important principle underlying all true prayer. All things in heaven and on earth exist for God's sake. The glory of God is the purpose of all that exists in all creation, and I do not hesitate to say that it is the *sole* purpose. You and I, all men, the righteous and the wicked, angels and devils, as well as all the wide creation must serve that one and highest purpose. Even all the work of salvation, with Jesus Christ in the center, is aimed at that purpose only. There are, even in this respect, no two ultimate purposes: the glory of God and the salvation of God's people. But the latter is subservient to the former. And it is the sole and full happiness and blessedness of the saved that they may forever willingly and consciously serve that purpose of their existence and calling. It is this truth that is embodied in the Lord's Prayer and that is revealed in the order of the two main groups of separate petitions, the first pertaining to God and the second to us.

How significant is this fundamental principle of all prayer!

How deeply and keenly we feel, as we compare our average prayers with the perfect model of the Lord's Prayer in this light, that we have as yet but a small beginning of that new obedience that enables us to pray!

What a close connection there is between a godly life and prayer!

For, let us not forget, this deepest principle of prayer does not mean that we seek God and His glory, His name, His kingdom, His will, first, and then, next to it and on a par with it, ourselves. But it implies that in our prayers we make all things subservient to that one supreme purpose: God and His cause. It means that we desire and seek and ask for our daily bread only in as far as it may be in harmony with His will, conducive to the coming of His kingdom, and tending to the glory of His name; and it means that we would rather go hungry in this world than that because of our bread God and His cause should suffer. It implies that we desire earnestly the forgiveness of sin, that we flee from and fight against all temptation, and long for the deliverance from all sin, because sin dishonors the name of God, is in conflict with the righteousness of His kingdom, and is opposed to the perfect will of our Father in heaven. How often is the disposition of our heart directly the opposite from what this principle of the Lord's Prayer requires it to be! How often are we inclined to seek our own ends, regardless of what may become of God's glory, His kingdom, and His will! Well may we humble ourselves deeply before the throne of grace. And well may we, after we have heard the Lord Jesus' injunction, "After this manner pray ye," get on our knees and earnestly beseech Him: "Lord, not only give us a model prayer, but above all give us grace to pray!"

We conclude this chapter with one more general and rather practical observation. We cannot fail to notice that throughout the perfect prayer the Lord teaches us to use the plural pronouns: *our* and *we*. *Our* Father, *we* pray that thy name be hallowed, thy kingdom come, thy will be done; *we* pray for *our* daily bread; *we* pray that Thou wilt forgive *us our* debts, as *we* forgive *our* debtors; and that Thou wilt not lead *us* into temptation, but deliver *us* from evil. And this does not mean that we may pray only in unison with all the people of God: we are admonished that we shall enter into our inner chamber, shut the door, and pray to our Father Who seeth in secret. Nor does it mean that we cannot have very urgent and pressing personal needs that impel us to cry to Jehovah very emphatically in the singular. The prayer of the publican must needs be in the singular: "God, be merciful to me, a sinner!" But it certainly signifies that true prayer presupposes love to the brethren and fellowship with all the people of God. Your prayer must needs die on your lips if you should appear in the sanctuary of God with hatred against the brethren, or even against one brother, in your heart. What the Lord Jesus once said with reference to offering one's gift on the altar applies with double force to the holy art of prayer, so that we may surely paraphrase His words thus: "If therefore thou art drawing near unto God in the sanctuary, and there rememberest that thy brother hath aught against thee, leave thy prayer unuttered, first go and reconcile with thy brother, and then return to offer thy prayer." (Matthew 5:23, 24)

May the Spirit of prayer and supplication give us grace to obey the injunction of our Lord, "After this manner therefore pray ye!"

Chapter 3

ADDRESSING OUR FATHER IN HEAVEN

"God is a Spirit: and they that worship him must worship him in spirit and in truth." (John 4:24) Prayer is always an act of worship. In all our prayers, therefore, this word of the Lord Jesus must be remembered and applied. It means that we cannot please the living God Who is a Spirit by mere outward form but that our prayer must be a matter of the heart. As we pray, there must live in our inmost mind and heart that which we express by the words of our mouth. We may flatter a man by vain words while our heart is far from him, but this is impossible with God. He looks at our hearts. Applying this truth to our discussion of the contents of the Lord's Prayer, we are constantly confronted by and must attempt to answer two questions. The first of these is: what is the meaning of each petition and of each part of this prayer? For we must pray intelligently, understanding what we say, and must not utter mere words that have no meaning for us. The second question we must seek to answer is: what is the spiritual attitude or disposition of the heart that is required in order to utter each petition in spirit and in truth? For if our spiritual disposition is not in harmony with the meaning of our petitions, we become hypocrites, abominable in the sight of God.

With these two questions in mind, we now consider the address, or allocution, of the model prayer the Lord left us, "Our Father who art in heaven."

"After this manner therefore pray ye: Our Father who art in heaven." Let us take notice, first of all, that these introductory words form no petition, but are the address of the whole prayer. Before we bring our requests to the throne of grace, we are taught to address, to speak to God directly and, as it were, face to face. What does it mean? What is the significance of addressing God in our prayers? Is the address intended as a mere form of politeness? Or does it serve some such purpose as the superscription of a letter?

It will be evident at once that it must have a much richer and deeper significance, especially if we remember that we must pray intelligently and that the spiritual condition of our heart must be such that we can utter this address in spirit and in truth. Then it will be clear that in this address we approach the true God, we come to stand before His face in the sanctuary. Then this address is not the thoughtless expression of what we have learned by heart, but the effort to conceive of Him as He is, as He revealed Himself to us, and to conceive of His relation to us. It is the spiritual exercise of faith whereby we seek and find Him, or rather, whereby we sought and found Him, that is expressed in this address. It is the expression of that spiritual activity of the mind and heart and soul whereby we are absorbed in profound contemplation of the living God, whereby we try to penetrate the darkness that envelopes us until we gaze with adoration and wonder upon His face and all our attention is concentrated upon His glorious majesty. Thus this act of addressing God determines our whole attitude throughout our entire prayer. It is because He is what we declare Him to be in this address that we direct our prayer to Him, that we dare to approach Him, that we are confident that He will hear us. And it is because we gaze upon Him, and keep the spiritual eyes of our faith fixed upon Him throughout our prayer, that we pray as we do and pray for the things we ask of Him. The address represents the indispensable preliminary of all true prayer, expressed in spirit and truth; it signifies that we have entered into the sanctuary and that we have found Him for Whom our soul is longing.

Simple, yet very profound, brief, yet all comprehensive is the address of the Lord's Prayer: "Our Father who art in heaven." Of course, the purpose of this allocution is not to impress upon our minds that we may never employ other words and other names of God than those of this particular address in our approach to the throne of grace. The particular circumstances under which we pray, the peculiar state of our mind and heart when we pray, and the specific consciousness of the needs we wish to present before the Most High — these often cause us to think of God particularly in the light of one or more of His infinite and marvelous virtues, whether it be His sovereignty or His omnipotence, His forgiving grace or His abundant mercy; and we address Him accordingly. But, first of all, these glorious virtues of God are all very really implied in this simple address of the Lord's Prayer. And, secondly, this address is certainly fundamental; and the attitude presupposed by it is surely indispensable to all true prayer. For if we cannot or dare not address Him as "Our Father," we cannot approach Him at all; and if we dare not add "Who art in heaven," we make Him like unto us, drag Him down from His excellency, and pray to an idol. As long as we must cry unto Him from the darkness of our present death and have not entered into the heavenly glory, we will never find an address to our prayers that is more perfect and all-comprehensive in its simplicity than that of the Lord's Prayer, acknowledging as it does the excellency of His majesty, while bringing Him very near unto us in His everlasting love.

If now we attempt to make a few remarks about the meaning of this address, the question arises, first of all: Whom are we taught to address in these words, "Our Father"? And the answer is, of course: the triune God, the one adorable Being of infinite perfections, Who is one in Essence, yet three in Persons, Father, Son, and Holy Ghost. By calling upon God as our Father, we do not speak to the First Person of the Holy Trinity, but to the one God subsisting in threeness of Persons. This triune God is the Father of creation, Who of nothing made heaven and earth. The same triune God is the Father of our Lord Jesus Christ, the Word become flesh, Who was delivered for our transgressions, and raised for our justification. Again, this same triune God is our Father for Christ's sake. It is true that we call upon Him as our Father through Jesus Christ His Son, and that it is only by the grace of the Holy Spirit that we can cry, "Abba, Father." Nevertheless, through the Spirit of God as the Spirit of Christ, and through our Lord Jesus Christ as the Mediator of God and man, we address not the First Person of the Holy Trinity, but the triune God when we say, "Our Father who art in heaven."

But what does it mean that we call Him our Father? It surely expresses that He made us His children. This is a profound mystery.
You can teach a small child to address God in the words "Our Father
who art in heaven"; yet the depth of truth expressed in these words is
not readily fathomed. For it implies that the infinite, glorious, adorable
God, Who is the implication of all perfections, a light in Whom there is
no darkness at all, so made us that there is in us an affinity and likeness
to the divine nature and, on the basis of this affinity, a communion of
life and a communion of love between Him and us. It signifies that He
made us after the image of His eternal Son, so that in a creaturely
measure we resemble Him and reflect His virtues of knowledge, righteousness, and holiness. It means that there is between Him and us the
living bond of love and fellowship, so that we can know Him, and trust
in Him, and believe that He will give unto us every good thing, and that
we delight in seeking His glory and in walking in humble obedience to
Him in the way of His precepts. Finally, it means that we have received
the right of children, the right to be called by His name, to claim His
care, to dwell in His house forever, and the right to the eternal inheri-
tance of glory which He prepared for all them that love Him. All this
is implied in the relationship between God and us that is expressed
in the words "Our Father."

Do not overlook the fact that in these two words he who prays and
thus addresses God is conscious of this relationship and confesses all
that is implied in it. He is consciously assured of his privilege to be
called a son of God. He feels in his heart that God is not ashamed to
be called his Father, and that He will not reject or repudiate him. He
is confident that he may approach God, that he may expect all good
things from Him, that he may dwell in the sanctuary of the Most High.
He is conscious of the fact that God has made him a reflection of His
own virtues, and that there is in his deepest heart a desire to be pleasing
to Him Whom he calls his Father, to be righteous as He is righteous,
holy as He is holy, and to keep all His good commandments. He trusts
that God loves him, and that He will surely give him all things necessary
for soul and body, and in the end eternal life in God's own tabernacle
forever. It is in that spiritual disposition of humble obedience, of

filial love and of childlike confidence that we approach the Most High in His sanctuary when we begin our prayers with the simple but profound address "Our Father."

But how is this possible? When did God bestow upon us the rights of sonship and make us His children? And whence do we have the assurance in our hearts that we are His children, the confidence to cry "Abba, Father"?

In this connection, many a modernist speaks of the universal fatherhood of God, and of the universal brotherhood of man, as if nothing happened to destroy that relationship since God created us after His own image. God is the Father of all men, and all men are children of God by virtue of creation. For man was made after God's image. That is his excellency above every other creature. That is his worth! On this fact of man's creation after the image of God modern man bases his right to life and liberty and the pursuit of happiness, his right, too, to enter into the sanctuary of God, and to address Him in the words "Our Father." But they forget the tremendous and terrible reality of sin and death. It is true, indeed, that God is our Creator, and that He made us after His own image, in true knowledge of Him, righteousness, and holiness. Adam was the son of God by reason of creation. (Luke 3:38) But no longer is it possible to call upon God as our Father on the basis of that original relationship. For by the fall and disobedience of the one man Adam, we lost the rights and privileges of sons; we were expelled from the Father's house, the image of God was subverted into the very image of the devil, and we are by nature the children of wrath. (John 8:44; Ephesians 2:3) And the result is that by nature we have no right, neither are we spiritually capable to utter the first two words of the Lord's Prayer in spirit and in truth. The modern philosophy of a universal fatherhood of God, which would place the address of this prayer upon the lips of every naked sinner without Christ, is sheer presumption, provocative of the fierce anger of the Lord. Would not even you be provoked to wrath and indignation, if a person from the lowest strata of society, notorious as public enemy number one, would spread the story everywhere that you were his father? How abominable, then, in the sight of God must be the pride

and presumption of the naked sinner, who walks in darkness and loves
iniquity, who reflects the image of his father the devil, and who, nevertheless, insists that he may take the son's prayer upon his lips and call
upon the Holy One as his Father!

   Not to the fatherhood of God in creation, therefore, but to that
far richer and deeper fatherhood which He revealed and realized in
Christ Jesus our Lord does the address in the Lord's Prayer have reference. The eternal Father of our Lord Jesus Christ is our God and Father
for His sake! That is the confession of him who humbly enters into
the sanctuary of God crying, "Abba, Father!" They who have learned
to pray "Our Father who art in heaven" do not boast of a universal
fatherhood of God. They speak of a very particular sonship, which
has its deepest source in eternal election, which has its firm ground
in the righteousness of Christ, crucified and raised from the dead, and
which has its efficient cause in the sovereign grace of God wrought in
their hearts by the Spirit of adoption. "Behold, what manner of love
the father hath bestowed upon us, that we should be called the sons of
God: therefore the world knoweth us not, because it knew him not."
(I John 3:1) God loved us with a great love. In that sovereign, elective
love He adopted us to be His children. He bestowed upon us the right
to be called the sons of God. This right can be realized for us in Jesus
Christ our Lord. For by His perfect obedience even unto the death of
the cross He obtained for us eternal righteousness, the forgiveness of
sins, and the adoption unto children. And in the resurrection of our
Lord from the dead we have God's own signature and seal to the cer-
tificate of our adoption. Not only so, but He also realizes this adoption
in our hearts. For he regenerates us, so that we are born of Him and
become conformed to the image of His Son. He quickens us unto a
new life. He calls us out of darkness into His marvelous light, so that
we repent of sin and long to be restored to His favor. He sheds abroad
in our hearts the love wherewith He loved us in Christ Jesus, and gives
us the faith whereby we rely on the righteousness of God in Christ
Jesus alone. And He causes the Spirit of Christ to dwell in us and to
abide with us forever, assuring us through the gospel that we are the
sons of God. For "when the fulness of the time was come, God sent

forth his Son, made of a woman, made under the law, To redeem them
that were under the law, that we might receive the adoption of sons.
And because ye are sons, God hath sent forth the Spirit of his Son into
your hearts, crying, Abba, Father." (Galatians 4:4-6) "For ye have not
received the spirit of bondage again to fear; but ye have received the
Spirit of adoption, whereby we cry, Abba, Father. The Spirit itself
beareth witness with our spirit, that we are the children of God."
(Romans 8:15, 16) It is, therefore, only in the name of Christ Jesus and
through the Spirit of adoption that we are able to say "Our Father."
And thus, at the very beginning of our prayer, the Lord leads us in the
marvelous way of God's grace and through the entrance of His sovereign election into the presence of the Most High! We may boast to man
of our own free will whereby we have accepted our sonship; but even
before we utter the first two words of the Lord's Prayer, this boast
has died on our lips, and we humbly confess: "Our Father Who art in
heaven, it is none of self, all of Thee!"

In these first two words, then, God Himself draws us very near unto
Himself, takes us into His bosom, and fills us with filial love and childlike confidence, so that we do not flee away from Him at the sight of
His glory and infinite majesty, but have boldness to remain in His
presence and to pour out our hearts before Him. However, this does not
mean that God now has become our equal and that henceforth we can
address Him with that familiarity that breeds contempt. There are
those who appear to think that it is a token of real piety that they
address the Most High very familiarly, as if He were their next door
neighbor. Thus I heard a well-known revivalist once introducing his
closing prayer with the words, "Oh, gee, Lord, I am tired!" It must be
evident that as long as anyone can express himself in such language, he
has never entered consciously into the presence of the most high
Majesty. He to Whom we speak in prayer is the same Whose glory and
majesty the prophet Isaiah beheld in a vision, "sitting upon a throne,
high and lifted up, and his train filled the temple. Above it stood the
seraphims: each one had six wings; with twain he covered his face, and
with twain he covered his feet, and with twain he did fly. And one
cried unto another, and said, Holy, holy, holy, is the Lord of hosts: the

whole earth is full of his glory. And the posts of the door moved at
the voice of him that cried, and the house was filled with smoke." And
as the prophet thus beheld the glory of the great God, he cried out:
"Woe is me! for I am undone!" (Isaiah 6:1-5) O, indeed, it is a marvelous privilege that we may dwell in the presence of that great God
and that we may confidently draw near to His bosom and stammer in
spiritual ecstasy, "Our Father." Let us beware that we do not destroy
the wonder of it by dragging God down to the level of our own existence! Our Father is the most high Majesty of heaven and earth. He
dwelleth in an inaccessible light!

Lest we should forget this, the Lord teaches us to address God as
our Father, but also to add immediately: "who art in heaven." We
understand at once, of course, that this addition may not be understood as a local, or limiting, qualification; and it is not designed to
make us cry very loudly to a very distant God, so that we may reach
Him with our voice. God is omnipresent. He is not only in heaven, but
also on the earth. "He is not far from everyone of us: For in him we
live, and move, and have our being." (Acts 17:27, 28) Even the very
heaven of heavens cannot contain Him. (II Chronicles 6:18) For He is
the transcendent One, infinitely exalted above all that is called creature.
Your prayer need not be a loud clamor to make Him hear you. When,
if occasion demands, in shop or office, in restaurant or train, you desire
to lift up your heart to Him in prayer, your whisper is quite sufficient;
and He inclines His ear even unto your silent prayer.

But there are especially two implications in the words "who art in
heaven." The first of these is that in your prayers you present yourself
to God as He is revealed in heaven, before His very face in Christ Jesus
our Lord. You do not address an abstract Providence, nor do you
speak to a vague Omnipresence when you pray. You seek Himself, His
face, His Person. Nor can you address Him as He is revealed on the
earth. For in our world "the wrath of God is revealed from heaven,"
and we lie in the midst of death. In His wrath we pine and die! But
in heaven, where the holy angels see His face, where is His sanctuary,
where He is revealed in the face of Christ Jesus our Lord, Who prays
for us with His continual intercession, there is the revelation of the

God of your salvation. Further, then, you direct your longing gaze. In your prayers you turn your eyes away from the present world and all that belongs to it, its wrath and death, in order to direct them to the holy place in heaven, whither Christ has gone before: for there you may find Him as your loving Father, at Whose heart you may find rest. And the second implication of the qualifying clause, "who art in heaven," is that God is very highly exalted above us and above all creation, infinite in power and wisdom, glorious in the splendor of His holiness. You shall not think earthly of Him, neither drag Him down from His excellency, but be filled with a holy reverence, even when you address Him as your Father. In this holy reverence and consciousness of His infinite power and wisdom you will, on the one hand, feel assured that He knows all your needs and that He is able to help you; on the other hand, you will refrain from praying thoughtlessly and from presenting before His face your sinful desires and carnal petitions. For thus the Scriptures admonish us: "Be not rash with thy mouth, and let not thine heart be hasty to utter any thing before God: for God is in heaven, and thou upon earth: therefore let thy words be few." (Ecclesiastes 5:2)

If you have followed this discussion of the address of the Lord's Prayer, you will agree with me when I say that, while it is quite possible to recite the entire Lord's Prayer in half a minute, it may well require a half hour of our time so to utter this address alone that through it we really lift up our hearts to the Most High, and contemplate Him with holy reverence, filial love, and childlike confidence. But if we have succeeded in this, and feel in our hearts that thus we have obtained audience with the living God, we are ready to pray. For in that holy reverence of Him that is in heaven, we will seek His glory above all, and all other things only for His name's sake. In that filial love of our Father we will be desirous to be pleasing to Him and ask only for those things that are according to His will. And in that childlike confidence we will feel assured that He will give us every good thing. For He is able to save us, being almighty God, and always willing to bless us, being our loving Father, Who "spared not his own Son, but delivered him up for us all." How, then, "shall he not with him also freely give us all things?" (Romans 8:32)

Chapter 4

HALLOWED BE THY NAME

First in the series of petitions which we are taught by the Lord's Prayer to present before the face of "Our Father" in heaven stands the request that God's name be hallowed. We must not overlook this position: for it teaches us at once that the chief and only purpose of all things is the glory of God, and that the desire for the realization of this purpose should be uppermost in our hearts and minds and should occupy, therefore, the first place in all our prayers. Unless we rightly know the name of God, we cannot pray to the true God at all; and unless the earnest desire that God's name may be hallowed occupies the chief place in our hearts, so that all our other desires are strictly subservient to it, we cannot ask anything that is according to His will. For of Him, and through Him, and to Him, are all things. Whatever may betide, therefore, to Him must be the glory forever! (Romans 11:36)

The name of God is His Self-revelation. God is God. We cannot find Him out. When in his sinful pride man refuses to be instructed in the knowledge of God from His own revelation and makes his own puny mind the measure of all things, it is inevitable that he reaches the conclusion that God is unknowable and that he is swallowed up in the quicksand of agnosticism and atheism. For God dwells in an inaccessible light. We cannot approach to Him. He is infinite, and we are finite: and the latter can neither comprehend nor establish contact with the former. He is the Eternal One, and we are children of the moment: how should time comprehend or reach out for eternity? If, therefore, we are to know God, He must reveal Himself to us: He must descend to the level of the finite, and there He must speak to us concerning Himself.

Briefly, this Self-revelation of God is His name. This name of God is
in all the works of His hands, in creation and history, and in the
wonders of salvation in Christ Jesus our Lord. For the psalmist sings:
"O Lord our Lord, how excellent is thy name in all the earth! who hast
set thy glory in the heavens." (Psalm 8:1) And again: "The heavens
declare the glory of God; and the firmament sheweth his handiwork.
Day unto day uttereth speech, and night unto night sheweth knowledge." (Psalm 19:1, 2) And again: "Unto thee, O God, do we give
thanks, unto thee do we give thanks: for that thy name is near thy
wondrous works declare." (Psalm 75:1) For all creation is His handiwork, and He made all things that they might be a revelation of His
marvelous virtues. They spell the name of the Most High. And not only
did He call them into being by the Word of His power in the beginning;
but He also continually dwells in them, sustains them, preserves them,
and governs them according to His eternal purpose. It is He that causes
the sun to rise every morning, that covers the heavens with clouds, that
"giveth snow like wool: he scattereth the hoarfrost like ashes. He
casteth forth his ice like morsels: who can stand before His cold? he
sendeth out his word, and melteth them: he causeth his wind to blow,
and the waters flow." (Psalm 147:16-18) And He governs with sovereign power the destinies of man and beast, of individuals and nations.
Hence, in all the world and in all its history we may behold the name
of God.

Yet, in this world of sin and darkness and death, we would never
behold the beauty and wisdom and full power of that name, and surely
could never know it as a name of salvation, had it not pleased Him to
manifest Himself to us in still another, a higher, a more glorious name, a
name of highest wisdom and power, of holiness and righteousness and
truth, of abundant mercy and boundless grace and fathomless love.
That name of God is revealed in Jesus, Jehovah-salvation, the Son of
God come in the flesh, Immanuel, God with us, Who fully revealed the
Father, Who bore our sins and bore them away forever on the accursed
tree, Who was raised from the dead on the third day and is seated at the
right hand of the Majesty in heaven, in Whom we have righteousness
and life eternal, and Who will come again in glory to become manifest

as the Head over all things in the new creation. That is the central and the highest revelation of Jehovah! In the light of that name we see the true meaning of the name of God in all the works of His hands.

Now it is the name of God as it is revealed to us and as we know it from the Holy Scriptures that is meant in the first petition of the Lord's Prayer, "Hallowed be thy name."

Let us notice that the Lord teaches us to pray that God's name be hallowed. Perhaps we had expected that He would rather have used the word "glorified." Yet, as we examine the meaning of the term "hallowed," we soon discover that it is both the deeper and the more comprehensive term, and that to glorify God presupposes that we hallow His name. The fundamental notion that is expressed by the word "hallowed" is that the name of God is holy, because God is the Holy One. This means that God is One, and that there is no god beside Him; that He is the infinitely perfect One, matchless in His infinite power, sovereignty, holiness, righteousness, truth, love, grace, and mercy; that He alone is consecrated to Himself, loves Himself, and seeks Himself; that He does all things only for His own name's sake; and that, therefore, all creation must be consecrated to Him and can be blessed only in as far as it serves the purpose of His glory. That He is the Holy One signifies that He is the Incomparable One, infinitely exalted above all that is called creature. He is Jehovah, the I AM, Who is eternally of and by Himself. He is God! Hence, His name is holy. It stands apart, by itself. It is a separate name. It has nothing in common with other names. It is the name of all names, by which all names exist in heaven and on earth. And when we are taught to pray "Hallowed be thy name," the Lord would have us say at the very beginning of our prayers: "Our Father who art in heaven, so reveal Thyself, and so let thy Self-revelation be acknowledged, that Thy name alone may stand out in all the world as a name of infinite wisdom and knowledge and power, of absolute Lordship and sovereignty, of unchangeable righteousness and truth, of matchless beauty, purest love, boundless grace, abundant mercy, as the only name that is worthy of all glory and adoration and praise forever!"

Such, briefly, is the meaning of this first petition of the Lord's Prayer.

But what are the implications of these words viewed as a prayer? For what do we ask when we take this prayer on our lips? For let us not overlook the fact that we are dealing here with a prayer. This is not the expression of a mere pious wish, "O, that thy name were hallowed!" We are asking for something. As we utter this petition, we are giving expression to a heartfelt need. We would like to receive some blessing from our Father in heaven. We earnestly beseech Him to do something in our behalf. What, then, is our request?

First of all, we are taught to beseech our Father in heaven that He will so govern all things — the affairs of the whole world, social, economic, political, national, and international; the affairs of His church in the world; and all things that concern us personally and our life in the world — in such a way that, first of all and above all, His name may receive all the glory and praise. For the Lord does not limit this petition, so that we merely ask our Father in heaven for grace that *we* may hallow His name. But He choses a general form, "Hallowed be thy name." This implies undoubtedly that the Most High will glorify His own name through us and through all things.

Now this is very significant. It means: "Father, glorify Thy name, regardless of what becomes of us, even though this should require that we be led in the ways of suffering and death. Glorify Thy name, O Father, no matter what becomes of our name!" It was thus that our Lord Himself prayed, when the dark shadows of the terrible cross were already stealing over His soul, and He said: "Now is my soul troubled; and what shall I say? Father, save me from this hour: but for this cause came I unto this hour. Father, glorify thy name." (John 12:27, 28) He was willing that the Father's name should be hallowed even though it would lead Him into the depth of hell. And we are taught in this first petition of the model prayer to pray for the same thing principally. That is why this petition stands at the head of the whole series of requests. The glory of God is first. The petition means that it is also first in our heart and mind. We seek that glory of God above all. In this petition we profess that we are not chiefly and first of all concerned about the question of what becomes of us and our earthly existence and life. If our Father sends war, and thus reveals

His name in the world, our first concern is not with ourselves and our earthly well-being, but that in and through the war God's name may be hallowed. Then we do not immediately and rashly cry for peace, regardless of what may become of the revelation of God's righteousness and power and holiness, but we say: "Our Father, even if it must be through war, glorify Thy name!" If we are led in ways of depression, hunger and want, suffering and sorrow, oppression and persecution for Christ's sake, we do not rebel against the ways of the Most High; but we humbly ask Him for grace to say: "Our Father, if I must be led through these deep and difficult ways in order that Thy glorious power and grace may be revealed, hallowed be Thy name!" Yes, indeed, this is the first implication of this petition. It means that we earnestly implore our Father in heaven so to reveal Himself that His name may be hallowed, whether it be in health or in sickness, in life or in death, in joy or in sorrow, in prosperity or in adversity, in peace or in war.

In the second place, this first petition of the Lord's Prayer also implies a request for grace that we may always hallow the name of our Father in heaven in our confession and in our entire life and walk in the world. Also this is significant, nor is it easy for us to learn thus to pray in spirit and in truth. For, mark well, this, too, implies that we earnestly desire grace from God always and everywhere to seek the glory of His name first, regardless of our position in the world.

This means, first of all, that we ask for grace rightly to know Him, Whom to know is eternal life. For how shall we glorify Him if we do not know Him with that true, spiritual knowledge which is the knowledge of love and fellowship and which is wrought in our hearts by His Spirit and Word? Again, this knowledge of God presupposes that we have the right and correct and full knowledge *about* Him. For how shall I know Him spiritually if I have no knowledge about Him, His name, His being, His virtues, His works, His salvation in Christ Jesus our Lord? This prayer, therefore, implies that we ask "Our Father" in heaven that He may give us the true, unadulterated knowledge, the right doctrine of Him. This true knowledge of God is contained in the Holy Scriptures. And we receive it and increase in it through the reading and searching of those Scriptures, as well as through the preaching of the

Word and through the instruction of ourselves and our children in that Word, in the home, in the school, and in the church. The first petition of the Lord's Prayer, therefore, implies that we invoke God's indispensable blessing upon all these means for the preservation and dissemination of the true knowledge of God. In it we pray that the church may be preserved and extended, and that she may receive grace to be zealous for the maintenance of the truth and grace to guard it against all error. We pray for its ministry, that it may be wholly devoted to the proclamation of the true gospel, both within the church and without, to the uttermost ends of the earth. We pray that, wherever our children receive their instruction, in the home or in the school or in the church, they may be nurtured in the fear and admonition of the Lord, so that they may become thoroughly furnished unto all good works. And then we pray that God may so sanctify the knowledge about Him unto our hearts by His Spirit and grace, that it may become true knowledge of Him in Jesus Christ our Lord. A thorough knowledge about God as revealed in the Scriptures is necessary, but a mere head full of doctrinal knowledge is not sufficient. This petition, therefore, also implies that we ask for God's Spirit and grace to give us that spiritual knowledge, that knowledge of the heart, which is eternal life, that we may love the Lord our God with all our heart and mind and soul and strength. "Hallowed be thy name" means: "Our Father who art in heaven, give us to know Thee more and more, and preserve us ever in the truth of Thy holy Word!"

What this means as to the spiritual disposition of our hearts that is required to send this petition to the throne of grace is not difficult to understand. It certainly presupposes that we are filled with an earnest desire and longing for the true knowledge of God, and that we employ every means to obtain that true knowledge. It means that we are not doctrinally indifferent, but that we are zealous for the truth as revealed in the Scriptures. For if this is not our attitude, we are hypocrites when we pray "Hallowed be thy name." And hypocrites are an abomination to the Lord! What would you think of a son who, being far from home, writes to his father that he longs to see him, but who does not even take the trouble of reading his father's letters? What, then, do you judge must be God's attitude to us if, while we pray with our lips that His name may be hallowed we plainly evince in our life that we are not interested in His Word? What of the preacher who from his pulpit sends this petition to the living God in heaven, but who proclaims to his flock his own philosophy instead of expounding to them the Scriptures and preaching the full counsel of God? What of the individual Christian who repeats this prayer, but who cares not for sound doctrine, if only his soul is saved, whose seat is usually vacant when God's people are congregated for worship, and who shows no interest in the preaching of the Word? What of the family that would pray for the hallowing of God's name, but in whose midst the Bible remains a closed book? What of parents who teach their children the Lord's Prayer, but who neglect to give them a Christian education? If such is our spiritual disposition and actual attitude when we take this first petition upon our lips, will not God answer us, "O you hypocrites and workers of iniquity, depart from me: for you honor me with your lips, but your heart is far from me"? Indeed, this prayer requires that we live in close contact with the Word of God and have a profound delight in the knowledge of His glorious name!

But we have not exhausted the meaning of this first petition.

For in it we also ask for His grace so to sanctify our hearts and minds that we may always glorify the name of our Father in heaven. To glorify Him implies, first of all, that we extol Him by the word of our mouth. And remember that we must glorify Him as GOD! We must not merely say some good things about Him, as if He were some man of renown. But we must confess and proclaim His infinite goodness, all His glorious and adorable virtues, His infinite power and wisdom, His glorious majesty and sovereignty, His righteousness, His justice and truth. We must praise Him as He revealed Himself to us as the God Who calleth the things that are not as if they were, and Who quickeneth the dead. We must adore His glorious virtues as they shine forth to us in the face of Jesus Christ our Lord, His unfathomable love, His abundant mercy, His sovereign grace. And, note carefully, to hallow His name, His holy name that stands apart from all other names, we must give Him *all* the glory and praise Him in *all* His works. We must beware lest we divide the glory that is due unto His name between Him and ourselves. For He is God! We never do anything for Him; He always does all things for us! His is all the glory of creation, of the government of all things, of salvation. Of Him, and through Him, and to Him are all things! Nor must we glorify Him and praise Him for some things which He does, while in other things we fail to see and acknowledge His infinite goodness. For His work is always perfect. In our whole life with all its vicissitudes, as well as in the whole course of the world's history and of the history of the church, we must see His work and adore His name. He sends prosperity, but also adversity; He makes peace, but war is also His; He gives health, but He also lays us on our sickbed; He maketh alive, but He also kills. Many of the details of His work we cannot now understand: for we are children of the moment, and from the viewpoint of our passing existence we cannot see the perfection of the whole of God's work. But believing His Word, we know that He doeth all things well and that He is always worthy of all praise and honor and glory forever. To hallow His name means that we express this praise, rejoicing in the God of our salvation; that we declare His glory to Him in prayer and adoration, in speech and song, and that we confess and proclaim His adorable virtues before one another and before all the world.

But to glorify God also implies that we manifest His wondrous grace in our walk. "Let your light so shine before men, that they may see your good works, and glorify your Father which is in heaven." (Matthew 5:16) To glorify God with our mouth but to walk in darkness is of the devil. The more piously we talk about God while we commit iniquity, the more abominable we become in the sight of God. The reason for this is not difficult to discern. Do we not confess that we are His workmanship, created in Christ Jesus? And does not the workmanship reflect the character of its author? Do we not confess that God is our Father, and do not the children reflect the image of their Father? If, then, we call Him our Father, while reflecting the image of the devil, do we not blaspheme His holy name? The prayer "Hallowed be thy name," therefore, does not only ask for grace that we always glorify Him in our speech, but also for His sanctifying Spirit that He may lead us in the way of His good commandments, so that our walk may be a reflection and manifestation of His glorious grace.

We have stammered a few words about the meaning of this first petition of the Lord's Prayer. The question now is: are we ready to pray after this manner? O, it should be abundantly clear by this time that this perfect model of prayer is not so well adapted for general use in public assemblies and mixed gatherings as it is often supposed to be, and that it is only the redeemed and sanctified child of God in Christ Jesus that can even begin to stammer it. But even so the question still is: Are *we* ready to say, "Hallowed be thy name"? Are we really earnestly desirous that He hear us and grant us our petition when we ask this of Him? Suppose He hear us: are we ready to receive this grace of Him? Are we prepared to say, "Our Father who art in heaven, glorify Thou Thy name in and through me, even though this should require that my name in this world should be completely eclipsed"? Do we really desire that He so instruct us by His Word and Spirit in the knowledge of His name that the zeal for its glory may consume us, and that His glory becomes our highest and only purpose in life? Do we really venture to ask Him for grace that we may always and everywhere confess and praise Him with our lips, and that we may constantly manifest ourselves as children of light? Do you realize that if God should hear this prayer, you may have to suffer reproach for His name's sake in the world, that it may cost you your job, your position, your very life?

If we are really children of God, we will answer: "Yes, I am ready to pray, but with fear and trembling. Lord, I believe: help Thou mine unbelief!" For we have but a small beginning of the new obedience by virtue of which we can pray. And as we presented this first petition before the face of our Father in heaven and somewhat realized its depth of meaning and tremendous significance, we probably feel that for the time being we have prayed quite enough, and that we may now properly close with the prayer: "Our Father who art in heaven, give us grace to pray, 'Hallowed be thy name.' Amen."

Chapter 5

THY KINGDOM COME

More, perhaps, than any other petition of the Lord's Prayer, the second in order, "Thy kingdom come," is in need of definition and clear exposition in our day. Many there are that speak of the kingdom of God, but they do not all refer to the same thing. Over against many voices that clamor for the kingdom of God as if it were a kingdom of this world, it is urgent that the church loudly and emphatically proclaim the testimony of the Word of God: "The kingdom of God is not of this world!"

Nothing is more common in our day than to speak of the establishment of the kingdom of God in every domain of human life. The kingdom of God must come in the state, in the domain of politics, in society, in national and international spheres. Its fundamental idea is that of righteousness among men: political righteousness, social righteousness, industrial righteousness, national and international righteousness. The possibility of its realization is given with the fundamental soundness of human nature and the universal brotherhood of man. This social kingdom-gospel is a philosophy that has borrowed almost all its terms from Scripture and from the faith of the church, but without adopting their essential meaning. It speaks of sin, but not as a corruption of the whole human nature, nor as a guilt that makes us damnable before God. It speaks of Christ, but not of the Christ of the Scriptures, Who was delivered for our transgressions and raised for our justification. It speaks of righteousness, but not of the righteousness which is of God by faith in Jesus Christ. It speaks of regeneration, but not of a radical change of the heart which is wrought by the Spirit of Christ.

Over against this beautiful and appealing, yet deceiving and vain

philosophy, it is well to state definitely the truth of Scripture and the
faith of the church concerning the kingdom of God. It is well to remind
ourselves that the kingdom of God is emphatically a kingdom of GOD,
not of man; that it is based on the righteousness of God in Christ, not
of man; that it is principally realized not by a man-made change in
human relationships, but by a divinely wrought redemption and regeneration of the individual sinner; that here in the world its sphere and
scope is not the universal brotherhood of man, but the fellowship of
the saints in Christ, the church of God; and, finally, that its perfect
manifestation and realization must not be expected in this world, nor
by way of gradual development, but by the final wonder of the appear-
ance of our Lord from heaven.

The kingdom of God, as to its main idea, is the commonwealth in
which God is King, in which He is known and acknowledged, loved and
freely obeyed by willing subjects as the only Sovereign of all. It is such
a rule of God as finds free and willing response in the hearts of the subjects of this kingdom. Upon this element emphasis must be placed. God
is, of course, always King. His dominion is an everlasting dominion, and
His kingdom ruleth over all. He rules over all the wide creation and over
every creature in heaven and on earth. No one can ever dethrone Him,
or even for a moment successfully dispute His sovereignty. He guides
the sun and moon and stars in their courses. He causes the heavens to
be covered with clouds, and the rain to satisfy the thirsty ground. He
clothes the forest with foliage green, and gives to the lily its garment
more beautiful than Solomon's raiment. The lightning and the winds,
the rivers in their course and the meandering brooks, the wild beasts of
the forest and all cattle, the cry of the young ravens and the song of
the lark — all alike are under the sway of His sovereign sceptre and obey
His divine will. Nay, more, He is also the sole governor of those
creatures that have a will of their own and consciously choose their
own way: men and angels. Even the demons and all the wicked of the
earth, though they rage furiously, and though they imagine a vain thing
against the Lord of all, can but execute His will and serve the purpose
of the realization of His good pleasure. God is sovereign forever and
ever. He rules by His power over all creation, and all creatures must

serve His purpose. But it is not this dominion that is meant in the prayer, "Thy kingdom come." In this kingdom He rules not by force, but by grace. He is enthroned not merely in the heavens, but in the hearts of the subjects. He has a covenant with His subjects, is their Friend, Who is known and loved by His subjects, who love to do His will and find their greatest delight in keeping His Word.

This kingdom of God is also the kingdom of Christ. For Christ, the Son of God in human nature, Who died for our sins on the accursed tree and was raised for our justification, Who is exalted at the right hand of God the Father, and Who will come again in glory, was anointed from before the foundation of the world to be the visible representative of the invisible God, the chief Servant of the Lord, as well as the Lord of all in the name of God, in this kingdom of God. In the heart of Christ is the spiritual center of this kingdom, and through the Spirit of Christ this glorious dominion of God is realized in the hearts of all the people of God. The kingdom of Christ, therefore, is God's rule through Christ, by His Spirit and Word. In and through Christ God laid the foundations of this kingdom in righteousness. Through Christ He makes Himself known to the subjects of this kingdom and all the glory of His grace. Through the Spirit of Christ He bestows upon the subjects of His kingdom all the spiritual graces necessary to enter into and to function in the kingdom of heaven.

For this reason, the kingdom of God does not extend any farther than the spiritual rule of Christ, which means that it is realized in the church. There is a close relation between the church and the kingdom of God, though there are also points of difference between the two conceptions. The church is the spiritual body of Christ; the kingdom is the commonwealth over which He rules. The church represents the house of God, His temple, in which God dwells with His people in most intimate covenant relationship; the kingdom emphasizes the idea of the servant-King relationship, in which God rules over us, and we delight to do His will. With relation to the church, Christ is the Bridegroom, the church is the bride; with relation to the kingdom, Christ is the King under God, and while doing His will, we reign with Him over all the works of God's hands. The church, as the bride of Christ, is also the new Jerusalem, the everlasting capital of the kingdom of heaven. And the church institute on earth serves the cause of the kingdom of God, especially through the preaching of the Word, the instruction of its members as citizens of the kingdom of heaven, and the gathering of all the citizens of the kingdom of God through the extension of the gospel to the uttermost parts of the earth. Nevertheless, the church and the kingdom are closely related. The members of the church are also the citizens of the kingdom, and the life of the kingdom becomes manifest only through the members of Christ's body. Both are the elect. They have their unity in the same Christ, the King of the church, the Head of the body. And they imply the same spiritual blessings of grace: righteousness and life.

Very often this kingdom is called the kingdom of heaven. This signifies that in no sense of the word is this kingdom of God a kingdom of this world. It has its origin in heaven, and always it comes down from heaven to overcome and replace the kingdom of this world. Even now it is in heaven: for it is centrally realized in Christ, Who sitteth at the right hand of God. And it is heavenly in its character, its blessings, and its glory. It is incorruptible, undefilable, and can never fade away because it has its center in the glorified Son of God in human nature. And it is not fully realized until in the new creation all things shall be united in Christ, the New Jerusalem shall have come down from heaven, and God shall be all in all, ruling through Christ and His church over all creatures.

Hence, until that day of Christ the kingdom of God is always coming, yet has never fully come. Once there was a kingdom of God on earth. This was in the dawn of history. For God made of the earthly creation a kingdom of God with its unity and center in the heart of man. Adam was formed after the image of God that he might rightly know his God, love Him, and be His friend-servant. And God gave him dominion over all creatures in the earthly creation. He was king. But he was a servant-king, a vice-regent. All creatures must serve him that with them all and before them all he might serve his God. In the heart of man the kingdom of God over all things was established. But Adam, the servant of God, rebelled and became disobedient. He apostatized from the living God, and allied himself with the devil. He became an enemy of God, guilty and corrupt, loving the darkness rather than the light. And instead of consecrating himself and all things to God as His servant, man now presses all things into the service of sin and unrighteousness. In as far, therefore, as man still occupies his position as king in relation to the earthly creation, he establishes a kingdom of darkness and unrighteousness which will reach its culmination in the kingdom of Antichrist, the man of sin, the son of perdition. This is the only kingdom that can ever develop in this world outside of Christ.

God, however, intended according to His eternal purpose to establish His dominion and realize His kingdom on a higher plane, the heavenly, and to lay its foundation firmly in Christ, the Son of God in human nature. For Him He had anointed as His eternal Servant-King; and in Him all things are to be united, both things in heaven and things on earth, to constitute the one, all-embracing kingdom of God. This kingdom of God in Christ is to come in the way of a battle in which the dominion of Satan, the kingdom of this world, the powers of sin, and death are to be completely vanquished. It is a battle, not for earthly dominions or material benefits or the rights of man, but for the righteousness of God, the acknowledgement of His sole sovereignty, and the glory of His name. The question is to be decided whether the Servant of God or the servant of the devil is to be king. In a sense, it may be said that this kingdom of God has been coming into this world from the very beginning of history. Its coming was announced in the so-called protevangel of Genesis 3:15: "I will put enmity between thee and the woman, and between thy seed and her seed; it shall bruise thy head, and thou shalt bruise its heel." There were representatives of this kingdom all through the old dispensation, representatives who embraced the promise and looked for the final victory over the powers of darkness, a victory that was held before them by the Word of God. A typical form of that kingdom was established in the theocracy of Israel, with its earthly king, its earthly throne on Mount Sion, its constitution in the Mosaic law and the covenant of Sinai, and its capital in the earthly Jerusalem. Centrally, the kingdom of God was realized with the first coming of Christ. The Son of God incarnate, the Babe

of Bethlehem, is the promised Seed of the woman, the seed of Abraham, the Lion of Judah's tribe, the Root of David; "and the government shall be upon his shoulder; and his name shall be called Wonderful, Counsellor, The mighty God, The everlasting Father, The Prince of
Peace." (Isaiah 9:6) He fights the battle for the kingdom of God alone
and lays the foundations of it when He becomes obedient unto death,
yea, unto the death of the cross, as the faithful Servant of Jehovah.
And the victory is given Him when He is justified and glorified in His
resurrection on the third day, His assumption into the highest heaven,
and His exaltation at the right hand of the Majesty in heaven. The
prince of this world is vanquished and cast out, and the kingdom of
God is realized in the glorification of the Son of God in human flesh.
All the shadows of the old dispensation are now become reality and
truth: Jerusalem, Mount Sion, the throne of David, as well as the
temple, the altar, and the perfect sacrifice, the King-Priest forever
according to the order of Melchizedec, all are in heaven. And all things
are subject unto our Lord, Who is the King of kings!

Still more. The kingdom of God is also realized in the spiritual
sense in the hearts of all the elect in the world by the Spirit of Christ
and the Word of God. For when God's people are regenerated, they receive the resurrection-life of Christ. And when they are efficaciously
called out of darkness into the marvelous light of God, they enter into
the kingdom of God. They become a royal priesthood. They share by
faith in the victory which Christ has gained for them. And in the consciousness of that victory, they fight the good fight of faith: not, indeed, in the hope that they can make a kingdom of God out of the
present world, but living the kingdom-life in every sphere of life and
representing the cause of the Son of God in the midst of a world that
lieth in darkness. Therefore, they put on the whole armor of God, considering it grace that, in the cause of Christ, they may not only believe
in Him but also suffer with Him. For they know that as citizens of the
kingdom of heaven they are still in Babylon. And in Babylon, in this
world, they do not expect an outward victory. They know that in the
world, they shall have tribulation: for as that world hated their King, so
they will hate them if they are faithful. They know, moreover, that

they must expect wars and rumors of war, earthquakes and famines, an increase in the might of the forces of darkness, and the final manifestation of the man of sin in the kingdom of Antichrist, in which there will be no room for those who refuse to worship the Beast and his image, and to receive the mark of the Beast in their right hand or forehead. Yet, in all this they fight and suffer with a good conscience, knowing that in the end they shall have the perfect victory. For still the kingdom of God is coming. It will come from heaven once again when the glorified Christ shall appear in all the splendor of His power, destroy forever all the powers of darkness, justify His cause and His people in the revelation of the righteous judgment of God, and establish His throne forever in the new heavens and the new earth, wherein righteousness shall dwell. Then the kingdom of God shall have come. God shall be all in all, our Lord Jesus Christ shall be Servant-King forever, and we shall reign with Him in glory over all the works of God's hands. In the final sense it is for this kingdom of heaven that we pray in the second petition, "Thy kingdom come."

If we have understood this brief exposition of the meaning of this second petition of the Lord's Prayer, we will be able to pray intelligently, without being confused by the many false philosophies concerning the kingdom of God that corrupt the truth in our day.

Then we will understand that this petition is, first of all, a request for something very specifically personal: we pray here for God's gracious rule in our hearts through the Spirit of Christ and by His infallible Word. It is, of course, the citizen of the kingdom of God, and none other, who sends and is able to send this request to the throne of grace. He is reborn. Christ snatched him from the dominion of the devil and established His throne in his heart. He is ruled by grace: sin has no more dominion over him. The law of God has been inscribed in his inmost heart, and he has a delight in God's good commandments. Yet he realizes very deeply that all this is true only in principle. He has only a beginning of the new obedience of the kingdom of God. He finds within himself the old ruts of sin, the sinful flesh. The motions of sin are still in his members. There is ever so much within him that rebels against the dominion of God's gracious rule in his heart and life.

Besides, he lives in the midst of a world that lies in darkness and that, by its vain philosophy, by its treasures and pleasures, by the lust of the flesh, and the lust of the eyes, and the pride of life, would seduce him to subject himself once more to the slavery of sin. And he is weak. In fact, in himself he is powerless to fight against those forces of darkness within and without. He knows that he is saved by grace, and that it is only by grace that he can overcome. He is deeply conscious of the fact that only in as far as God rules over him by His grace and Spirit and through His Word, can he remain and manifest himself as a citizen of the kingdom of God. Knowing all this, and understanding, too, that God surely gives His grace and Spirit to them that ask Him, he prays: "Our Father who art in heaven, more and more rule over me by Thy Spirit and Word, over my heart and mind, over all my thoughts and desires, in order that I may not become conformed to this world, but be transformed by the renewal of my mind. Thy kingdom come within me!"

But this petition also implies a prayer for the church. For it is the church of Christ that represents the kingdom of God in the world and through which the cause of the kingdom is preserved and extended. By that church the gospel of the kingdom is proclaimed, the truth of the kingdom is preserved and taught. Within the church the children of the kingdom are born and nurtured. And through the ministry of the church the citizens of the kingdom are called from the uttermost ends of the earth. Hence, the prayer for the kingdom of God includes a prayer for the church. In it we ask that the Spirit of Christ may so rule in the church that she may be preserved in the midst of the world, that she may be founded in the truth, and that the false philosophy of the world may not seduce her, that she may grow in the knowledge and grace of the Lord, that the preaching of the Word may be kept pure and unadulterated, that she may remain faithful in the midst of all forms of temptation and persecution, that the covenant of God may be continued in the line of her generations, and that through the preaching of the Word even in heathen lands the elect may be translated out of the kingdom of darkness into the kingdom of God's dear Son. And this presupposes that spiritual disposition of the heart according to which the church, the true church, where the Word of God is maintained in all its fulness and purity, is above all things in the world dear to us, that we diligently seek its fellowship, and that for no carnal reasons we will ever separate ourselves from its communion, so that we can truly sing with the church of the old dispensation: "If I forget thee, O Jerusalem, let my right hand forget her cunning. If I do not remember thee, let my tongue cleave to the roof of my mouth; if I prefer not Jerusalem above my chief joy." (Psalm 137:5, 6) Preserve and extend Thy church, O God, and destroy all her enemies! Thy kingdom come!

Finally, this prayer means that we ask and long for the coming of the day of Christ, when all the elect shall have been gathered, when Christ shall appear in glory, the dead shall be raised in incorruption, the present world shall pass away, all the forces of darkness shall be destroyed forever, new heavens and a new earth shall be created, and the kingdom of heaven shall be established in eternal perfection. "Thy kingdom come!" Yes, indeed, that means that ultimately we pray for the coming of Christ and for all that it implies. We know that He will come through wars, and pestilences, and famines, and earthquakes. We know that the hastening of His day will mean that the measure of iniquity must be filled, that Antichrist must be revealed, that we shall have to suffer for His name's sake. We know that, praying for the coming of the Lord, we must condemn the idealism of a sinful world, as if a lasting peace can ever be established before His coming. Yet we pray, "Thy kingdom come!"

Or do we? Do we not feel, now we begin to understand the real implications of this second petition, that also in this respect we have but a small beginning of the new obedience, and that we are often too earthly-minded, too much engrossed in seeking the things that are below, to send this petition to the throne of grace in spirit and in truth? Well may we, even before we take this prayer on our lips, earnestly beseech the Lord to teach us to pray, and say: "Our Father who art in heaven, give us grace to pray, 'Thy kingdom come! Come, Lord Jesus!' Amen."

Chapter 6

THY WILL BE DONE

How intimate and beautifully conceived is the relation between the first three of the petitions of the Lord's Prayer, and how perfect is their unity. At the head of them all stands the petition that the name of God may be hallowed and that thus the highest and only purpose of all things may be clearly revealed and realized. But if that supreme aim is to be attained, the works of darkness must be destroyed, and that perfect state of things must be inaugurated in which God alone rules by His Word and Spirit, and He shall be all in all. And the praying Christian, realizing this, expresses his heartfelt need and desire in the second petition, "Thy kingdom come." And when that kingdom shall have come in all its power and perfection and glory, God will be all in all, and His will shall be done in earth as it is in heaven. But as this perfect state is still a matter of the future, and there still is a difference between earth and heaven, the believer is taught to continue his prayer, "Thy will be done in earth, as it is in heaven."

In this petition, then, our attention is called to the will of God. God is a willing Being. He is not an impersonal power like the wind, or a blind force which we call fate. He is an intelligent and volitional, personal Being. He is a willing Being in the absolute sense of the word, and as such He is sovereignly free. All He does He wills to do, and all He wills He sovereignly performs. There is the most perfect harmony between God's Being and His will. He never does anything involuntarily, still less by compulsion, or contrary to His own will. With us this is quite different. Our actions may be distinguished into voluntary and involuntary actions. When I speak, or sing, or pray, I perform voluntary actions. But when I breathe, or when someone unexpectedly stabs a knife into my flesh and I cry out, I perform actions which are quite involuntary. Then, too, we often do things which we would not like to do if the choice of them were left entirely to the decision of our will, but which we decide to do nevertheless, because necessity is upon us. But there are no such involuntary actions and conflicts in God. His Being and His will and His acts are always in perfect harmony with one another. God is a willing God in the absolute sense of the word. "He hath done whatsoever he hath pleased." (Psalm 115:3)

Because of this perfect harmony, the will of God is always good. For God is good. His Being is the implication of all infinite perfections. He is truth and righteousness and holiness. He is a light, and there is no darkness in Him at all. There is no evil in the Most High. And, as His will is always in harmony with His Being, and as there are never any conflicts in God at all, it follows that His will is always characterized by absolute perfection. God can never will anything sinfully. His will is eternally opposed to all evil. He abhors all iniquity. He is light. He dwells in the light. He wills and has His eternal delight in the light. This does not mean that sin and evil exist in the world without His will, as powers in themselves, which He could not prevent and over whose entrance into the world He had no control. If we know and believe the Bible, we know better. That God is absolutely sovereign, also with respect to sin and evil and all the powers of darkness, Scripture teaches us very plainly. For He declares in Isaiah 45:7, "I form the light, and create darkness: I make peace, and create evil: I the Lord do all these things." But even when it is His sovereign will and counsel that evil shall exist, His will is righteous and holy. For always He wills it unto the realization of the highest purpose: the glory of His name. Even when in His eternal counsel He gives a place to sin and evil, it is always the object of His divine hatred, and never can it be said that God has delight in evil. The will of God is always good.

In what we just stated we touched the distinction between the will of God's counsel, or decree, and the will of His command, or ethical will. The same distinction is often expressed by the terms *secret* and *revealed* will of God. God's decrees are called the secret will, while the will of God's command is designated as His revealed will. These terms, however, are not quite correct; and they are often the occasion of a serious misunderstanding. On the supposition that God's counsel is secret the contention is often based that we are not at all concerned with it: the secret things are for the Lord our God, the revealed are for us and our children. We know nothing about God's eternal counsel; and, therefore, we do well if we do not curiously inquire into its hidden depths. Surely, it is said, they are to be condemned as erring dangerously who place the truth of God's eternal purpose in the foreground as a basic doctrine.

Clearly, however, this is not correct. It is true, of course, that there are secret things. The details of God's purpose are hid from us. We do not know the day of our death, nor the way we must still travel before that day arrives. No one can predict how long the present war will last, nor what will be the outcome, or what is the purpose it must serve in the divine plan.[1] We know not what tomorrow will bring, and every day is sufficient unto the evil thereof. Further, we can know nothing of the will of God's counsel except what is revealed of it in the Scriptures. But this does not mean that we may simply dismiss the truth of God's eternal purpose from our mind and ignore it in our preaching and instruction. God revealed His counsel to us. The fact of the eternal good pleasure of God, as the sovereign and unchangeable purpose according to which He works all things in time, is certainly not hid, but clearly revealed; and it occupies an important, a basic place in Scripture. Moreover, the general lines of that eternal counsel are clearly drawn in the Bible. God wants His people to know His counsel with respect to salvation and with regard to all things, in order that they may speak of it and be witnesses of His wisdom and power and absolute sovereignty.

We prefer to speak, therefore, of God's will of His decree and His will of command. God's decrees are His eternal and sovereign thoughts and determinations concerning us and concerning all things; His decree is the will which He Himself executes and realizes in the history of the world. His will of command, however, declares what His moral creatures

---

1 The reader is reminded that these chapters were originally radio messages, delivered in the early part of World War II.

must be, and will, and do. It pleased God to create beings which have a will of their own, rational, moral creatures. They are creatures which are capable of knowing "what is that good, and acceptable, and perfect will of God" (Romans 12:2), and that in all their acts consciously function in relation to that will. And the will of God's command reveals to these moral creatures, men and angels, what and how they shall think and will and desire and act, so as to be in harmony with His own righteousness and the objects of His favor and delight.

Now to what does the third petition refer? It teaches us to pray, "Thy will be done in earth, as it is in heaven." Does it refer to God's will of decree, or to the will of His command, or, perhaps, to both? Do we pray here that God's counsel may be realized, or that we may obey the will of His command? Or is it impossible to separate the two, and are both implied in this prayer?

It is rather usual to explain that in the third petition of the Lord's Prayer the reference is exclusively to the will of God's command, so that the meaning is: give us grace that we may always do Thy will and keep Thy good commandments. God's counsel He Himself performs. We do not. And He performs it perfectly: His counsel shall stand, and He will do all His good pleasure. There is, therefore, no sense in praying that His will of decree may be done. Besides, the Lord adds to this petition: "in earth, as it is in heaven," meaning, evidently, that as in heaven His will is perfectly obeyed, so it may also be on the earth. It must be evident, therefore, that this prayer has reference only to the will of God's command, and that the will of His counsel is not included in the scope of this petition.

There is truth in this contention. The main thought of this prayer is, indeed, that God's will may be perfectly obeyed. However, it should be clear that in our actual life we can never separate the will of God's command from that of His decree, and that, while obeying His will and keeping His precepts, we are constantly in contact with the execution of the will of His decree. In other words, if we obey the Lord our God and walk before Him according to His good commandments, we must constantly learn to will His will of decree as it is realized in our life. Let me use an illustration to make this clear. Suppose that God sends the cold hand of death into our home to snatch away a dear child. In doing so He executes His own eternal purpose. That child is torn away from our heart according to the will of God's decree. Of course, with the execution of this will of God's decree concerning us we have nothing to do. God takes the child, and our will has nothing to do with it. And yet in another sense it has a good deal to do with this revelation of the purpose of God to us. We must certainly learn to will the will of God in the death of that child. There is, in connection with this revelation of the will of God's decree, a very special way in which we must walk, a very special calling which we must fulfill: the calling to submit ourselves to the will of God, yea, to blend our will with His, yea, to give Him glory and praise even in the midst of our sorrow according to the flesh, and to confess that He does all things well. In this particular case the third petition of the Lord's Prayer would mean: Lord, give us grace that in this particular way in which Thou leadest us, we may walk in complete surrender to Thy holy will, so that we may be able to say from the heart, "The Lord hath given, the Lord hath taken away; blessed be the name of the Lord." (Job 1:21)

Thus it is with the whole of our life. Always we must find and obey our calling in the particular place in which God stations us and in the way in which He leads us. The clearest and most profound illustration of this truth we have in the prayer of our Lord in Gethsemene, where He, too, sent this petition to the Father, "Thy will be done." He prayed then in the agony of His soul. The dark shadow of the cross stole over His soul. He was, as He told His disciples, exceedingly sorrowful, even unto death. He clearly anticipated the full horror of the way that stretched out before Him that night. Already He tasted the bitterness of the cup He had to drink in obedience to the Father as the perfect Servant of Jehovah. And He was sore amazed. So perplexed He was that even in that extreme hour he conceived of the possibility of some other way of obedience than the one in which He was about to descend. And He poured out His soul before the face of the Father in that darkest of nights, and prayed: "Father, if it be possible, let this cup pass from me; nevertheless, not my will, but thy will be done." To be sure, the Lord Jesus here prayed that He might be obedient to the will of the Father even unto the end: He would drink the cup His Father gave Him to drink. In that sense His prayer referred to the will of God's command, the command that He should lay down His life for the sheep whom the Father had given Him. Yet how closely this obedience of the Savior was connected with the will of God's eternal counsel concerning Him. God had decreed the way of the cross in all its horrors and sufferings for His only begotten Son. And it was in the way of that counsel that the Lord had to become obedient to the end.

It is no different with us. To be sure, the prayer "Thy will be done in earth, as it is in heaven" emphasizes that we may do His will perfectly as it is obeyed by the inhabitants in heaven, the perfected saints and the holy angels, with Christ in their midst and at their head. It would hallow all our earthly life and consecrate it to the living God. It teaches us to consider the whole of our earthly life, in all its different phases and departments, as a calling, an office, a mandate, and ourselves as office bearers, servants of the living God. For the will of God concerns our whole life. In all of our life, we who have been called out of darkness into His marvelous light are His servants, called to do His will. We cannot divide life into two main departments, or spheres, so that we serve God in the one, but consider that the other lies wholly outside of the sphere of His will. All of our life belongs to Him. Always and everywhere we are in His service. Our whole existence is an office. With the life of our body and that of our soul, with our mind and all our desires, in all the various relationships of life, in the family, in society, in shop or office, in church and state, we are called to serve Him; and always we must ask for that "good, and acceptable, and perfect will of God." Thus all life is hallowed by this third petition. The minister in his pulpit, the elder in the oversight of the flock, the deacon in his work of mercy; yes, but also the teacher before his class, the policeman on his beat, the shoemaker at his bench, the mother in the daily routine of her homely tasks, the father at the head of his family, the children in relation to their parents — everyone, without exception, whatever his station in life, finds that the will of God governs his life and must be obeyed. The prayer "Thy will be done in earth, as it is in heaven" teaches us to look upon all of life as a calling of God in which we must glorify our Father in heaven.

But let us not overlook that in thus seeking to know and to do the will of our Father in heaven, we are, as it were, encompassed on every side by the will of His decree. For our stations and calling, our way and our circumstances are not all alike. They vary greatly. The one is rich, the other poor. One is of high, the other of low estate. The one has received many talents and gifts from God, the other few; and there are those who receive but the one talent. Accordingly, our positions in life differ. This is true even in the angel world. Gabriel stands before God; Michael is a prince among the angels; and there are powers and principalities in heaven. No less is this true on earth. Some hold an exalted place, others perform the lowlier tasks of life. There are kings and rulers, and there are those who dig sewers and clean the streets. In the church some are ministers of the gospel, others are elders or deacons, still others are Sunday-school teachers or leaders in the various societies, while the great majority function simply in the office of believers. Now whence comes this difference in gifts and talents, in station and calling? It comes from God, Who governs our entire life according to His eternal good pleasure. And in that particular station and calling which He assigns to us we must be His servants and walk in obedience to His good and perfect will. And so we see that in our entire life there is a close relation between the will of God's counsel and the will of His command, and that somehow they are both implied in the prayer "Thy will be done in earth, as it is in heaven."

For what, then, do we pray in this third petition?

First of all, we are taught here to beseech our Father in heaven for grace that we may always accept our position in life as our particular assignment from Him, and our way as the way He ordained for us, in order that in that position and in that way we may function as His servants and do His will. Oh, we need grace, much grace, grace every day to assume that attitude! How inclined we are to divide life into separate spheres: a sphere of our religious life, in which we serve the Lord and clearly think to discern a calling and office, and a sphere of our everyday life, which we may probably mix with some religious exercises, but in which we fail to consider ourselves servants of God who must ask for and do His will. In that case we look upon our daily work, whatever that may be, as something rather profane. We conduct our business in order to make a living, or to accumulate wealth. We look upon our work in the factory as a necessary evil. The housewife goes through the daily routine of her work as a kind of drudgery. The teacher is glad when the day's toil is over. We distinguish between a calling and a job. A minister of the gospel has a calling, but outside of that most people simply have a job. That to work in the shop or to dig sewers, to make tools or to build a house, to bear children and to bring them up, to darn stockings and to wash dishes, or whatever may be the work that is awaiting us every day — that these also belong to our calling from the Lord, how many of us think of it and live accordingly? Yes, so it is! The Christian has been called out of darkness into God's marvelous light and has been liberated from the slavery of sin in order that with his entire life in all its relationships he might be taken into the service of his God. Hence, wherever he is stationed and in whatever way God leads him, there he must see his calling. Well may he daily ask for grace that he may accept his position without murmuring and look upon it as a calling from his Father in heaven. "Thy will be done! Grant, O Father in heaven, that I may always and everywhere live as before Thy face, in the consciousness of my calling to be Thy servant."

Then, in the second place, in this petition we ask for grace that in that particular calling which is ours, we always be ready to do the Lord's will, even though this should mean that we have to renounce our own will. For to do the will of God in our whole life means that we shall be diligent in our work, that we shall be honest in our business dealings, that we shall be kind and just to those who are in our employ, provide good working conditions for them and pay them a fair wage, that we shall be in subjection to those who have the rule over us, obeying them not as eye-servants or men-pleasers, but as serving the Lord Christ. In short, it implies that we shall consecrate ourselves with all our powers and possessions and means unto the God of our salvation, and that we shall walk as children of light in the midst of a world that lies in darkness, confessing the name of the Lord and glorifying our Father which is in heaven. It means that we fight sin within us, forsake the world, and walk in all good works day by day and every-

where. For the prayer is that we here on earth may perform the will of
God as faithfully and perfectly as the inhabitants in heaven do His
will. The Lord directs our eyes to heaven here once more. There is
Christ, the perfect Servant of the Lord; there are the saints who have
gone before and who are delivered from the last vestige of sin; there are
the holy angels who hearken to the word of God's mouth and are ever
ready to execute His will. That so perfectly and so cheerfully and gladly
we may do the will of our Father in heaven is the request in this third
petition of the Lord's Prayer. "Our Father in heaven, teach me Thy
will to know, and from the heart Thy will to do!"

Finally, also this prayer looks forward to the consummation of all
things, to the perfect life in the New Jerusalem, in the new heavens and
in the new earth, in which righteousness shall dwell. For the prayer that
God's will may be done in earth as it is in heaven certainly looks forward to the state in which the workers of iniquity shall be no more, in
which all, without exception, shall do the will of God. You understand,
of course, that also in that new creation each one will have his station
and calling. We are not just going to sit down lazily on the banks of
the river of life, singing our songs and playing our harps. On the contrary, the perfect life will be full of activity and work. Only then there
will be no more toil, and no more slaving for a living or for filthy lucre.
All our work will then be service of God, fully and consciously! For
that final perfection the believer longs. Here he finds that even his best
works are defiled with sin, that often he is inclined to rebel against the
Lord because of the way he must travel or the place he must occupy.
Besides, here he comes into daily contact with a world that cares not
for the will of God, that is full of unrighteousness and rebellion, and in
which it is ever so difficult to do the will of his Father. And then
looking upward to heaven, where even now the will of the Most High is
the delight of all, he longs for the time when all life in all the new
creation will be like that in heaven. And prostrating himself before the
throne of grace, he prays: "Our Father, who art in heaven, give unto
me, give unto all Thy people Thy Spirit and grace to know and to do
Thy will; and hasten the day when the workers of iniquity shall be no
more, and when all shall be in perfect harmony with Thy will, which
is only good. Thy will be done! Amen."

Chapter 7

THE PRAYER FOR BREAD

The fourth petition, the prayer for daily bread, appears to be so earthly in its contents that all men without distinction may take it on their lips. It would seem to require no special spirituality to send this request to the throne of our Father in heaven. Here is a prayer that touches a deeply felt need of every man and woman on earth; and surely even the natural man can pray, "Give us this day our daily bread." Thus many think, but they are very much in error.

Rooted in the same erroneous conception of the content of this fourth petition is the opinion of some over-spiritual Christians that in this prayer we have no request for material bread at all, but that the Lord teaches us here to pray for spiritual nourishment, for the bread that came down from heaven. From the lofty heights of their would-be spirituality, these people judge that it would be below the high level of this perfect model of prayer to insert a request for mere bread, for earthly necessities. They argue further that if this were the meaning of the fourth petition, it would stand in flat contradiction to all that the Lord teaches us elsewhere concerning our attitude towards earthly things. For He admonishes us that we shall not ask, "What shall we eat? or what shall we drink? or wherewithal shall we be clothed?" All these things do the Gentiles seek, not the citizens of the kingdom of heaven. Besides, our heavenly Father knows that we need these things. We must therefore seek the kingdom of God and His righteousness, and for the rest simply trust that all these things shall be added unto us. (Matthew 6:26ff.) How, then, could it be possible that the same Lord would insert a prayer for these very things in the series of petitions which He teaches us to pray?

67

We will not take the time to enervate these arguments and refute them. The simple words of the petition, its exact position in the series of prayers we are taught to pray, as well as the reminder that we are still on the earth and not yet in heaven — all this ought to be sufficient to convince anyone that we do, indeed, have a request for daily, earthly, material bread in this fourth petition. But we do wish to emphasize, in opposition to both views mentioned above, that, even though we deal here with a prayer for very tangible bread, the petition is nevertheless very deeply spiritual. This is not a common petition, which any man can pray. The natural, unregenerated man certainly is not able to make it his own. All the manifestations of greed and covetousness, the strife after the things of this world and always more of them, the constant and bitter fight between the haves and the have-nots, the lust of the flesh, and the lust of the eyes, and the pride of life — all these constitute a striking contrast to the simple request in this fourth petition.

But even for the believer it is not always easy to utter this petition in spirit and in truth without reservation. We do not usually live on the high spiritual level that is required to take this petition on our lips and mean it. And the end also of the present meditation on the Lord's Prayer will have to be an acknowledgement on our part that we still have much to learn and that we will have to assume an attitude of constant watchfulness in prayer to be able to say, "Give us this day our daily bread."

Let me call your attention, first of all, to the fact that this petition occupies a secondary place in the Lord's Prayer. In the second section of this model, which is concerned with our own needs, it has a leading place, on the basis of the principle that the natural is first, even though it is not most important, while the spiritual is second in order. In the order of time, we need bread even before we need the forgiveness of sins and the deliverance from evil; and as soon as we need bread no more, we shall have no more need for forgiveness and deliverance. But although it occupies the first place in this second section, we must not overlook the fact that together with the whole of this second part of the Lord's Prayer, it is strictly subordinate to the first part, in which we are instructed to ask for the glory of God's name, the coming of His kingdom, the submission to and obedience of His will. The significance of this is clear. It means, to be sure, that in the fourth petition we pray not simply for bread in order that we may eat and drink, still less in order that we may use the bread for the satisfaction of our sinful desires, but in order that we may be able to hallow the name of God, to seek His kingdom, and to obey His will. "Give us bread, our Father, that we may serve and glorify Thee, and represent Thy cause in the world" — thus we are taught to pray.

But this order teaches us something else. The statement is often made quite without reservation that in this prayer we have the promise that God's people in this world will never lack bread, will never suffer hunger, that every day their food and drink will be provided. Now in the sense that the Lord will always care for His people, and that He will provide them with the necessary means to live as His people in the world, this is true. But we should not forget that all this is strictly subservient to the purpose of God's glory, the coming of His kingdom, and the realization of His will. Scripture teaches us everywhere that we must expect suffering for righteousness' sake in the world. And this suffering may very well include that the portion of our daily bread becomes very small, that we suffer hunger and want, starvation and death. The apostle Paul relates how for the kingdom of God's sake he was "in weariness and painfulness, in watchings often, in hunger and thirst, in fastings often, in cold and nakedness." (II Corinthians 11:27) And the Epistle to the Hebrews mentions those who "wandered about in sheepskins and goatskins, being destitute, afflicted, tormented." (Hebrews 11:37) And does not the Bible forewarn us that the time shall come when we shall not be able to buy or sell, unless we receive the mark of the beast? (Revelation 13:17) It is important, therefore, that we bear in mind that we pray for our daily bread in strict subordination to the glory of God's name, the coming of His kingdom, and the realization of His will which is always good.

Turning our attention to the contents of this petition, we are at once impressed by the fact that it places the petitioner on the level of a very simple life as far as earthly things are concerned. It teaches us to ask for bread, no more. We understand, of course, that there is a figure in this term. It represents more than mere bread. We need more. Clothing and shelter and all the necessities of our earthly life are represented by "bread." But it is very evident that "our daily bread" definitely excludes whatever is above and beyond the things that are strictly necessary for our physical and earthly subsistence. One cannot very well so stretch the term bread in this petition as to include riches and luxuries. Especially in modern life we have a thousand and one things for our enjoyment: delicacies to please our taste, luxuries to make life pleasant, conveniences to render our earthly life comfortable. But these are certainly not included in the fourth petition. This is not saying that we may not have them if we are sure that our heavenly Father gave them to us, and that we may not enjoy them if we can do so with thanksgiving. But it does teach us that we may not set our heart on these things, that we may not seek them, covet them, and that, therefore, we may not ask our heavenly Father for them. Positively speaking, it teaches us that we shall seek and ask for only those things that are strictly necessary for our earthly subsistence. In the fourth petition we do not pray for riches and for an abundance of earthly goods. We do not pray for sugar and coffee, for cake and pie, for beautiful clothes, for comfortable homes and radios and pianos and automobiles. The fourth petition with its request for bread puts us on a very simple level of living: "Give us bread!"

This same idea is emphasized still further by the word that is translated "daily." Give us this day our *daily* bread. The Greek word that is translated by our "daily" presents a little difficulty, and there is considerable doubt as to the exact meaning of the term. The problem is that in the New Testament it occurs nowhere else. However, it may be said confidently that it does not mean *daily*. Some suggest that the word means "that which is present." The meaning of the prayer, then, would be "Give us this day bread for the present." But this idea is really already expressed in the words "this day." Give us *this day* our bread means: give us bread for the present. Others see in the composition of the original word the meaning *coming* or *future*. The Lord then would teach us to pray: "Give us this day the bread that is coming, bread for the future, for the morrow." But this would appear to be in direct conflict with the teachings of our Lord when He emphasizes that we shall not be anxious for the morrow, and that one day is quite sufficient as to its own evil. To me it seems that the word may properly be rendered by "bread that is coming to me." The prayer then means: give us this day the bread that is coming to us, i.e., the bread that is our proper portion for this particular day. Give us our own, proper, limited portion of our daily necessities. This proper portion varies. It is not always the same, nor is it the same for all. The needs of a large family with small children differ from those of an old couple. Those needs are different on a severely frosty day in January from what they are on a pleasant, warm day in June. They are not the same when we are sick as when we are in good health. Our proper portion varies according to our circumstances and position in life. And the prayer asks that our Father in heaven in His wisdom may give us that particular portion which is proper for us.

We should not overlook the further limitation of this proper portion of bodily necessities expressed in the words "this day." This is to be taken most literally and most seriously. It does not mean that we may ask for a well-stocked food cellar, a full coal bin that may carry us through the winter, or a reasonably large bank account on which we may fall back. It does not imply that we ask our Father in heaven to give us so much that we may feel secure for a year, for a month, for a week, or even for another day. It means exactly what it says, "Give us what we need for this day." In other words, the prayer teaches us to assume the attitude which the Lord exhorts His people to assume with respect to earthly things: "Take therefore no thought for the morrow: for the morrow shall take thought for the things of itself. Sufficient unto the day is the evil thereof." The morrow is not ours: for we are but children of the moment. To ask for today is sufficient. And if, as the dusk of evening settles upon our earthly life of the day, we have neither bread in the house, nor the means wherewithal to buy bread even for another day, but the Lord did provide for us in the day that has come to its close, He heard our prayer and fulfilled His Word: "Give us this day our proper portion of bread."

Now the believer is taught to turn directly to his heavenly Father to ask for this proper portion of bread for this one day.

This means, first of all, that we acknowledge His sovereignty and power over all things and our own dependence on Him, and on Him alone. He is the Lord of hosts, and His kingdom ruleth over all. In whatever way, and by whatever means, and through whatever channels we may obtain our daily bread, we boast not in self, in our own ability and strength and wisdom, nor in men and an arm of flesh, but acknowledge the sovereignty of God. Let us make no mistake. This is not a prayer adapted only for the poor, who must live day by day. It is a prayer just as well for the rich. It is not meant only for those who must kneel down by their empty bread baskets every day to ask the Lord of all to fill them. It is a petition that must be sent to the throne of grace also by those who sit down by their well-supplied tables, loaded with an abundance of food. For that food is not ours. It is our heavenly Father's. He must give it to us. He prepared it. He supplied us with it. He brought it to our tables. This is true, no matter what may be our position in the world. It may seem easier for the farmer than for the industrialist to utter this prayer. For it is rather evident that God sends the rain and the sunshine, that He gives the increase and makes the corn ripen in the field. But it may appear more difficult how God brings the loaf of bread to the table of the shop worker, through all the maze of economic and industrial and commercial relationships that exist in our world. Yet the believer knows that even over all these relationships His Father in heaven rules and that He governs them absolutely. Whether the wheels of industry shall be idle or busily spinning, whether there shall be labor for our hands or whether we shall be without employment, whether we shall be able to work and provide for ourselves and those who are dependent on us — all these things depend not ultimately and really on us, or on the wisdom or ingenuity of man, but on the Lord our God in Christ Jesus our Savior. And the child of God is taught to acknowledge his dependence on no one but his Father in heaven when he is enjoined to pray, "Give us this day our daily bread."

Of course, this prayer presupposes that we do not strive anxiously or greedily to secure our bread in a way that is contrary to the will of God. If one would idle his time away, neglect his calling, be lazy and refuse to labor for his daily bread, and then send this petition to the throne of our Father in heaven, he would thereby tempt God, and his prayer would not be heard. Or if one accumulates riches in a way that is contrary to the will of our Father in heaven, by false dealing or usury if he is a businessman, by cutting the wages of those who are in his employ if he is an employer, by forcing his employer to raise his wages by strikes and boycotts and violence, by speculation or gambling or other illegal methods; or if one has abundance, and knows that his brother is poor, and fails to provide for him; or if he piles up his savings for a possible "rainy day" while he refuses to provide from his portion for the needs of the kingdom of God in the world — he is a hypocrite when he kneels down to pray, "Give us this day our daily bread." For this prayer surely implies that the believer would receive his daily bread only from the hand of his Father, in His own way, and, above all, in His favor.

Thus, if we have understood the real implications of this fourth petition, we will be ready, too, to acknowledge that this prayer, though it places us on the level of a very simple earthly life, and exactly because of this, would have us live on a very high spiritual level. It is not necessary any more to make special mention of the fact that the natural man, the unbeliever, the world, cannot possibly take this petition on his lips. The world is quite directly opposed to all that this prayer teaches us with respect to the attitude we are supposed to assume toward earthly things. The unbeliever does not want just bread; he is not satisfied with his portion of bread; above all, he wants more than bread for *this day*. He wants the world. He wants abundance. This is true not only of the rich, but also of the poor. All the strife and unrest in the world testifies to the fact that the spirit of the world is opposed to the spirit of the fourth petition. The world strives after what in our day is rather profanely styled "the more abundant life." And how could it be different? The natural man understands not the things of the kingdom of God. He does not acknowledge himself to be in the service of God with all things, to be a mere steward with respect to earthly things. He serves the world. He seeks the world. His slogan is "Let us eat and drink, for tomorrow we die." He has no hope beyond this world. He does not know the transcendent joy expressed in the confession "Thy loving kindness is better than life." Small wonder, then, that he serves Mammon. And in that service one surely cannot pray, "Give us this day our daily bread." And let us not overlook the fact that the wicked, too, eats his bread, and that he usually eats in abundance. God often gives him more of it than He gives His own children. But He gives it to him in His wrath. By the abundance of worldly goods He sets the wicked on slippery places, on which He casts them down into destruction.

> Although the wicked prospered seem,
> At last they vanish like a dream
> And perish in a day;
> Jehovah's foes shall soon appear
> Like fields once fair, now brown and sear;
> Like smoke they fade away.
>
> (*Psalter* Number 97:3)

However, with the child of God, who has been called out of darkness into light and who lives by faith in the Lord Jesus, his crucified, risen, and exalted Redeemer, all this is principally different. For, first of all, he has been called back into the service of the living God; and so the things of this world are for him not an end in themselves, but a means to an end, the capital entrusted to him, that with it he may serve his God. He does not live to eat and to drink and to be merry, but he eats and drinks to live, and that, too, to live in the service of God. Secondly, having been translated into the kingdom of God's dear Son, he seeks the kingdom of God, the things which are above, where Christ sitteth at the right hand of God. He knows that God is not ashamed to be called his God: for He has prepared for him a city, the heavenly city that has foundations. Here, he knows, he lies in the midst of death, and in the midst of death eats his bread. But he looks forward to the glory of his risen and exalted Lord, the heavenly Jerusalem that shall come down out of heaven from his God. In that faith he knows himself to be only a sojourner, a stranger, and a pilgrim in this world. He is content to live in tents. He does not lay his foundation deep and strong, and build magnificent houses in this world. He must travel. He cannot tarry. And living in tents, having his eye fixed on the city that has foundations, he is satisfied day by day to receive that portion of his daily bread which is sufficient for him to continue the journey. And so he prays, every morning, as he pulls up his stakes to resume the journey: "Our Father in heaven, give us this day our daily bread."

Already you have understood that this petition presupposes that spiritual disposition that is expressed by the Scriptural term "contentment." The apostle Paul writes to the church in Philippi: "I have learned, in whatsoever state I am, therewith to be content." (Philippians 4:11) Contentment is that spiritual virtue according to which my inner state of heart and mind is always in harmony with the will of God concerning me as realized in my earthly way. In that state I am satisfied with my lot, knowing that it is from God, and that He will cause all things to work together for my good. There is an expression of contentment in the fourth petition. In it we do not ask for great things. By it we express before our Father in heaven that we shall be satisfied with the bare necessities, content to live on the level of the most simple earthly life. We declare here: "Our Father which art in heaven, if it please thee to give me more than is strictly necessary for me to continue my journey this day, I will be satisfied and receive it from Thy hand with thanksgiving." This also implies childlike confidence. I live by the day. I am not anxious for the morrow. If I have nothing left tonight, and I know not how I shall obtain breakfast tomorrow, I shall not worry, but lay me down to sleep, confident that my heavenly Father lives tomorrow as well as today, and that He will care for me. "Give us *this* day our daily bread, and we shall not be anxious about the morrow."

Realizing, however, that this is the spiritual disposition required to utter this petition in spirit and truth, we at the same time feel that we are still far from that spiritual perfection. How carnal we often are! How we, too, are inclined to seek the things that are below! How little of the pilgrim attitude becomes manifest in our lives! How often we murmur against the will and way of the Lord! And how little do we evince of that spirit of childlike confidence that expects all good things from the God of our salvation! Well may we conclude also this meditation on the Lord's Prayer with the humble request: "Lord, give us grace to pray, 'Give us this day our daily bread.' Amen."

Chapter 8

FATHER, FORGIVE!

In the structure of the Lord's Prayer the fifth petition, the prayer for forgiveness, occupies a perfect position. It is worthwhile to consider this place for a moment. First of all, if we have understood the real meaning and implications of all the preceding petitions, the very exercise of sending them to the throne of grace must have awakened within us a deep sense of our imperfections and sins, and therefore deepened our feeling of need for the forgiveness of our sinful condition and of our actual transgressions. How often we do seek things quite different from those which we professed to seek in the first three petitions of the Lord's Prayer! How small is the principle of perfection within us by virtue of which we always seek the glory of God's name first and above all! How frequently we are seeking the things that are below rather than the kingdom of God and His righteousness! And how we are inclined to rebel against and to transgress the will of our heavenly Father rather than keep it perfectly! But this does not only apply to the first three petitions. Also while we stammered the prayer for bread, we felt our lack of faith and confidence, our sinful anxiety for the morrow, our lusting after the "fleshpots of Egypt." If therefore we have uttered these petitions in the sanctuary, before the face of God, in spirit and in truth, we should be quite ready now to pray, "And forgive us our debts."

In fact, even apart from the erroneous conception on which such a view is based, it is rather impossible to understand how there can be true Christians, or those that profess to be such, who claim that there is no longer any place for this prayer in the life of the child of God, that to pray this is a manifestation of ignorance or an expression of unbelief.

They emphasize that all prayer for forgiveness really belongs to the old dispensation. Now, however, Christ has come, has died on the cross, and through His blood has blotted out all our sins. Our sins, therefore, are forgiven once and forever; and it is really a denial of the cross of Christ to pray now, in the new dispensation, for the forgiveness of our sins. I say: even apart from the doctrinal error implied in such statements, it is rather difficult to understand how a true child of God, who knows himself, is able not only to make such statements, but to live according to them, that is, without the prayer for forgiveness. For to me it seems that every day the Christian must feel the need exactly of this prayer and that, as he grows in the grace and knowledge of Jesus Christ, this need will become deeper and this prayer will grow more intense. Even in those times when his spiritual life is at low tide and when he does not feel much need of prayer, it would seem that the burden of this petition still lies heavily upon his heart: "And forgive us our debts, as we forgive our debtors."

Let us note two more characteristics of the peculiar position of this petition in the structure of the whole. First of all, it follows the prayer for bread. This is in accord with the principle that the natural is first, "afterward that which is spiritual." (I Corinthians 15:46) Our daily bread is not more important than the forgiveness of sins, but it is first in order of time. Only in this world, and therefore only as long as we need bread, are we in need of forgiveness. Secondly, this prayer for forgiveness precedes the petition for grace against temptation and for deliverance from evil. This, too, reminds us of an important truth: justification must needs precede sanctification. We must have forgiveness before we can be and before we even can have the right to be delivered from the bondage of sin and from the dominion of the Evil One. On the other hand, even while we pray for forgiveness, we bear in mind that the petition for deliverance from sin immediately follows: for how could we possibly pray for forgiveness unless there were in our hearts the sincere longing for complete deliverance from all evil and for spiritual perfection?

In trying to understand the meaning of this fifth petition, various questions present themselves. What is sin? What is the forgiveness of sin? How is forgiveness of sin possible at all, and what is its ground? Precisely what is the meaning of that limiting clause "as we forgive our debtors"?

These questions we shall now try to answer.

We are aware, of course, that in the gospel narratives there are two versions of the Lord's Prayer, the one in Matthew 6 and the other in Luke 11. The former occurs in the Sermon on the Mount; the latter was given in answer to a request by the disciples that the Lord would teach them to pray. Now in these two versions two different words for "sin" are used in the petition for forgiveness. In Matthew we find the word that is properly translated by our English word "debts"; in Luke we find a word that is most commonly used for "sin" in the Bible and that denotes an aiming at the wrong mark, a striving after the wrong purpose, missing the mark. We may well combine these two meanings into a single conception, for they belong together. To begin with the last-mentioned term, it implies that God has so created us that in all our actions we are engaged as rational, moral creatures, and that there-fore we must have an aim, a purpose for which we strive, a reason why we do things, an inner motive that urges us to act. It also presupposes that God has appointed for man the purpose for which he must strive in all that he does, and the motive by which he must be actuated in his whole life. God sets before man the mark at which he must aim. That purpose is, of course, the highest end of all things, for which, however, man must consciously and willingly strive: the glory of God. In all his life, inner and outward, in his thinking and willing, his desires and aspirations, in his speech and actions, in his personal life and in his relationship to others and to the whole creation, man has the calling to strive for the glory of God. This also implies that he must be actuated by the pure motive of the love of God. That, then, is the mark at which man must aim. The word for sin which we are now discussing means, in the third place, that the sinner is missing that mark, not by accident or in ignorance, not in spite of the fact that he exerts all his effort to aim at it, but willfully and deliberately. We are enemies of God by nature, and we will not seek the glory of God. We deliberately aim at something else, our own glory, the satisfaction of the lust of the flesh, and the lust of the eyes, and the pride of life. That, then, is sin. Whatever forms sin may assume, in its deepest sense it always means not to live from the love of God, but deliberately to aim at another mark, to strive for another purpose than the glory of God. And so we become debtors with God. This is the meaning of the word used in Matthew. Sin is debt. By not reaching the mark in all our life, we come into arrears with God. We did not meet our obligations with the living God. And the more we sin, the higher we pile up our debt.

Now in this fifth petition we pray that God may forgive us our debts. What does that mean? We ask God to do something with our sins. What?

The word used in the original for "forgive" really means to send away, to dismiss. That is significant. For it denotes that forgiveness is something very wonderful and that the prayer for forgiveness is a very bold, an amazing request. It means that we implore God to dismiss our debts! This implies, first of all, that He dismissed them from His own heart and mind, so that He will never recall them again, never make mention of them anymore; that He completely obliterates them from His book of remembrance, so blots them out that they can never be found any more. It means that God will never hold it against us that we have always missed the mark, always trampled His glory under foot, always violated His good commandments. Yes, but it means more: for we cannot appear as neutral persons in the judgment of God. It signifies something positive. It means not only that God will not impute our sins unto us, cancel our debts, but also that He will judge us righteous and so consider us as if we had always been nothing but obedient children who never once transgressed His holy law. And so this prayer to dismiss our debts implies, secondly, that God will not at all be angry with us for having missed the high mark of our calling, the glory of His name. We know that our sins are a fact. We are aware that God is terribly displeased with all sin. But we ask Him so to dismiss our sins from His mind that He will never be angry with us. Again, this also has a positive meaning: for God's attitude toward us cannot be neutral. In this petition, therefore, we ask for God's favor, His lovingkindness, His blessed friendship. "So dismiss our debts that they never provoke Thy holy wrath against us, and thus consider us righteous that we may be the worthy objects of Thy favor!" Such is the meaning of this petition. Finally, it follows that forgiveness means that God does not treat us, that He does not deal with us as sinners in His wrath, but that He treats us as righteous in His eternal favor. For in His wrath He must needs curse us; but in His favor He will bless us with all the goodness of His house, eternal life. And so this prayer means: "Our Father, who art in heaven, be pleased so to dismiss my sins that I may be righteous when Thou judgest me, may be the object of Thy blessed favor, and may be found worthy of the glory of eternal life."

But notice now that this is emphatically a *prayer* for forgiveness. That means that I ask for something. I do not merely request that God do something, that He cancel my sins and blot them out, that He dismiss them from His own mind; but I want an answer to my requests. I desire a gift for myself. I ask for a gift of grace in this fifth petition. The gift for which I ask is the forgiveness of sins. I want to have it, to possess it, to be assured of it in my deepest heart, that God has so forgiven, dismissed, cancelled my debts, and so clothed me with eternal righteousness that I am still the object of His favor, and that He gives me eternal life! I want to have that blessed gift of the forgiveness of sins *now*, at once, in this world, while I am in the flesh, in which everything testifies against me, condemns me, speaks of wrath and death and hell. I want it, not as something that will deliver me from the guilt of sins I may have committed in the past, but even while I am still sinful and while I am sinning! That is the amazing wonder and boldness of this petition. I do not say: "Father, last week I sinned, or yesterday I sinned, or this morning I sinned: please, forgive." But I say: "Father, I am sinning all the time, I am sinning even at this very moment while I am praying; please, dismiss my debts from Thy book, and clothe me with righteousness in Thy judgment! And, Father, I must have an answer: please, give me the unspeakably blessed assurance and peace of forgiveness in my heart!"

Now this is a great wonder. We are, of course, very much used to the idea, or at least to the sound of the words "forgiveness of sins." Perhaps we are so accustomed to it that we hardly ever feel the amazing marvel of it all. Yet, a great wonder it is; and in this fifth petition I ask the Lord for grace and faith to lay hold on God's own wonder of redemption: the death of His only begotten Son. For in the mystery of the cross of our Lord Jesus Christ alone is found the ground of the forgiveness of sins, and in that cross only can we conceive of the possibility of this prayer. For it may sound very paradoxical, but it is a fact, nevertheless, that forgiveness must be an act of strictest justice on the part of God. It is an act of boundless grace and abundant mercy, to be sure, but of mercy that itself is strictly just. God is holy, and righteous, and unchangeably just. He cannot deny Himself. And, therefore, all His acts are truth and justice, also His acts of grace and mercy. If then the sinner is ever to receive forgiveness, this act of God's great mercy must be based on strictest righteousness. In other words, if the sinner is to be forgiven, he must be justified. Now how can a sinner be justified before God? Only by expiation of his sin. Sin must be blotted out. But how can sin be blotted out? Only by an act of atonement.

What is atonement? The heart and essence of atonement is satisfaction of God's righteousness with respect to sin. And what may satisfy the righteousness of God with respect to sin, so that the sinner is truly justified before God? Only such an act of perfect obedience, of the obedience of love, whereby the sinner bears the full wrath of God against sin in all its implications and consequences willingly. In other words, if the sinner willingly, obediently, from the love of God, descends into the suffering of deepest death, and thus sacrifices himself on the altar of God's righteousness, he thereby expiates his guilt and becomes righteous before God. But this the sinner can never do. If he could, he would need no forgiveness. But this is forever impossible. The sinner is an enemy of God, and he can only increase his debt with God daily. And this is the unfathomable mystery of the love of God, not that in justifying the ungodly He winks at sin and sets aside His justice, but that in the Person of Immanuel, His only begotten Son in our flesh, He Himself accomplishes this act of perfect obedience for the expiation of our sins. "For God so loved the world that he gave his only begotten Son, that whosoever believeth in him shall not perish, but have everlasting life." (John 3:16) And: "God was in Christ, reconciling the world unto himself, not imputing their trespasses unto them." (II Corinthians 5:19) That is the mystery of the cross! In the moment of the cross God forever blotted out all the sins of all the elect. They are justified. Their sins are no more. And it is on the basis of the atoning, justifying act of God in Christ that our sins are forgiven us.

But how shall we lay hold on this mystery of reconciliation? How shall we obtain for ourselves the forgiveness of sins? How shall we, who are still in the midst of death, who sin daily, receive the assurance in our hearts that our sins are forgiven us?

The only possible answer to this question is this: we can lay hold on the mystery of the cross and the resurrection of Christ, and therefore on the forgiveness of our sins, only when God Himself by the Spirit of Christ, and through the Word of the gospel says to us, "Your sins are forgiven you!" We must hear God Himself speak to us through the gospel. This is possible only through faith, which He Himself gives unto us, and which He alone through the Spirit of Christ can bring to that conscious activity whereby we lay hold upon the blessing of forgiveness. And so you understand that it is all of Him, none of self. His is the blessing of reconciliation through the blood of Christ. His is the Word of justification through the resurrection of Jesus Christ from the dead. His is the Spirit of Christ through Whom He applies the grace of the Lord Jesus to our hearts. His is the gospel of reconciliation through which this amazing wonder is proclaimed to us. His is the knowledge of sin and the true sorrow after God that causes us to need and to cry out for forgiveness. His, too, is the faith and the activity of faith whereby we may and do lay hold on this abundance of grace. And so the prayer is born in the heart of the believer, a prayer to which he must have an immediate answer, a prayer, not of unbelief or of doubt, but exactly of faith: "Our Father who art in heaven, forgive us our debts!" And the answer to this prayer, thus wrought by grace in our hearts, thus uttered by faith and in true sorrow after God, surely comes, and comes at once. Unless it come, you cannot utter another word. Unless you hear it, you must needs flee from the presence of God. But it surely comes, by the Spirit of Christ and through the Word of the gospel: "Thy sins are forgiven thee!"

But note now the very serious limiting clause which the Lord adds to this prayer for forgiveness: "as we forgive our debtors."

You understand, of course, that this cannot mean to express a ground for our plea for forgiveness. We do not make ourselves worthy of forgiveness by forgiving one another. But for the rest, we must take this clause very seriously. Does it really mean then, you probably ask, that God will not forgive my sins if I do not forgive the brother that sinned against me? O, yes! It means exactly that. It means nothing else. God will give unto us the grace of forgiveness only as we also forgive one another. The Lord emphasizes this point very strongly. He even singles it out and puts it in bold relief. At the close of this prayer as we find it in the Gospel according to Matthew, we read this special explanation of the fifth petition: "For if ye forgive men their trespasses, your heavenly Father will also forgive you: But if ye forgive not men their trespasses, neither will your heavenly Father forgive your trespasses." (Matthew 6:14, 15) And at the close of the well-known parable of the unmerciful servant, the Lord warned: "So likewise shall my heavenly Father do also unto you (that is: deliver you to the tormentors until you have paid the uttermost farthing!), if ye from your hearts forgive not everyone his brother their trespasses." (Matthew 18:35) If, therefore, you appear with this plea for the forgiveness of your sins before the face of God, you must be quite sure that there is no one toward whom you assume an unforgiving attitude, lest the Lord deliver you to the tormentors!

But this does not exhaust the meaning of this limiting clause.

We must note that there is a comparison here: "Forgive us our debts *as* we forgive our debtors." This means that we fashion our forgiveness of one another after the model of God's forgiving our trespasses, and that we are so conscious that we have actually done this that we are now able to pray that God may forgive us in the same manner as we have forgiven one another. This implies several ideas. It means that our debtors desire forgiveness, are sorry for their sins committed against us, and confess their wrongdoings. Only in the way of repentance and confession can we obtain forgiveness from God; and only in that same way can we forgive one another. It means more. Perhaps you are strongly inclined to agree with our last remark; and being rather of an unforgiving spirit, you decide to wait until the brother who sinned against you will come to humble himself before you. But you must remember that God did not wait until you came to Him; but He came to you, while you were enemies of God, dead in trespasses and sins, and by His grace He quickened you and led you to repentance. Hence, you cannot afford to wait, but must seek the offending brother and seek to bring him to repentance. Further, it means that we forgive one another abundantly. There is never an end to God's forgiveness. Never does God say to us: "So often have I forgiven you, and always you commit the same sins: I will forgive you no more." There is never a last time with God. He forgives abundantly. His mercy is without limit. So also there can be no last time with us. Always again must we forgive the brother who repents, and that, too, for Christ's sake.

The reason for all this, let me repeat, is not that our forgiving of one another is a ground for our prayer for forgiveness: for that is Christ and His atoning blood absolutely alone. But in order to receive forgiveness of God I must have receptivity for that blessed gift of grace: I must be truly sorry for my sins, and I must behold and long for the unspeakable mercy of God in Christ. And all this is not present as long as I am assuming an unforgiving attitude to the brethren. There is no more unmistakable sign that I have no true need of forgiveness, and that, therefore, I am in no condition to receive it from the Lord, than that I shut up my heart against the brother and assume an attitude of unforgiving pride over against him. If we love not the brother whom we have seen, how can we love God, whom we have not seen? With what measure ye mete, it surely shall be measured to you again. Hence, it is quite impossible to beseech the Lord for forgiveness, unless we can truly add: "as we forgive our debtors."

We will now be able to understand what spiritual disposition is required to utter this petition in spirit and in truth. There must be true sorrow over sin, over sin as such because it offends God, over *all* sin without exception. There must be a sincere desire to be completely delivered from all sin and to walk before God in true obedience. There must be confidence, not in self, but in the blood and resurrection of

Jesus Christ alone, as a ground for our prayer. And there must be love of the brethren and the sincere desire to forgive one another. Considering all this, we must no doubt confess that also in regard to this petition we are still far from perfection. How thoughtlessly, superficially, and insincerely we often express the words of this petition! And yet it is only in the measure that we truly and consciously send this petition to the throne of grace that we can taste the joy of forgiveness and can exclaim with the psalmist: "O the blessedness of the man whose transgression is forgiven, whose sin is covered!" (Psalm 32:1)

"Lord, teach us to pray! Amen."

Chapter 9

THE PRAYER AGAINST TEMPTATION

The prayer for forgiveness of our sins cannot possibly be the last of our petitions. It looks forward to something else, to a better, a higher, a more blessed state, in which the prayer for forgiveness shall never again be necessary. In the prayer for forgiveness we seek to lay hold on the glorious gift of justification through the blood of Christ. This justification, the act of God whereby He forever declares us free from sin and clothes us with an eternal righteousness that is imputed to us on the ground of the perfect sacrifice of Jesus Christ our Lord, is very important. It is basic for all other blessings of grace. It is first. But it is not last. Justification changes our legal status before God in judgment, but it leaves our sinful condition unchanged. It delivers us from the guilt of sin, but it leaves us still stained with the pollution of sin. By it we obtain the right to be delivered from the dominion and power of sin, even as the pardon of a governor gives a criminal the right to be set at liberty. But it does not itself liberate us from that power. Hence, justification, the forgiveness of sins, cannot be the end of salvation. For Christ did not give Himself for us merely in order that we might be redeemed and justified, but that He might "purify unto himself a people for his own possession, zealous of good works." (Titus 2:14) Objectively, therefore, justification is the ground of sanctification. We are justified in order that we may be sanctified; we are pardoned in order that we may be liberated; we are forgiven in order that we may be delivered from the power and pollution of sin.

Now even as in an objective, doctrinal sense justification looks forward to sanctification, and the former is the ground of the latter, so subjectively, in the application of these blessings of grace to the elect and in the experience of the believer, the two are most intimately related and may never be separated. In the life and consciousness of the Christian, justification never exists alone, without sanctification. In fact, we may even say that in principle the believer is made holy before he can ever lay hold on the blessing of the forgiveness of sins. It is the regenerated, called, and believing Christian who longs for, seeks, and receives his justification in Christ our Lord. It is the beginning of a sincere love of God and the consciousness of a deep sorrow after God that makes him cry for forgiveness. But by the same token, the prayer for the forgiveness of sins cannot be his final request with respect to sin. As long as he is in need of the prayer for remission, he has not reached perfection; he is still sinful and still transgresses the good commandments of his God in thought, word, and deed. With this condition he cannot be satisfied. The very same sorrow after God which makes him bemoan his sins and impels him to cry out for forgiveness also causes him to hate sin, to realize the danger of falling into temptation while he is in this world, to seek strength to fight against the powers of evil within him and round about him, and to long and pray for the state in which he will be completely delivered from the dominion and corruption of sin and will serve his Father in heaven in perfect righteousness. The petition for forgiveness, therefore, already looks forward to and must needs be followed by this other prayer, "And lead us not into temptation, but deliver us from evil."

The question whether in these words we must find one or two petitions we will leave undecided. Some favor the latter view, and thus discover seven petitions in the Lord's Prayer. Others insist that the former view is correct and that the perfect prayer contains only six separate requests. The question is a purely formal one, and of minor importance. It must be admitted that from a formal viewpoint everything is in favor of the view that in these two clauses we have one request. They form one sentence, connected by the conjunction "but." The whole sentence runs parallel to the fifth petition, which also consists of two clauses. Besides, there is a very close relation between preservation in and from temptation and deliverance from evil.

It may be expedient at this time to look at that relation a little more closely. Some understand the connection between the two parts of this prayer in such a way that the last part of the petition makes provision in case the first part of this prayer is not granted. The meaning then would be: "Lead us not into temptation; but if we must be led into it, then deliver us out of the evil." However, this quite arbitrarily introduces a thought into the text which is foreign to it. Besides, it presupposes the possibility that the first part may not be heard. This interpretation, therefore, must be rejected: for "without faith it is impossible to please God; for he that cometh to God must believe that he is, and that he is a rewarder of them that diligently seek him." (Hebrews 11:6) Rather must we conceive of the relation to be such, that in the two clauses of this prayer we ask for the same blessing of grace, the first part expressing the thing asked for negatively, the last clause positively. "Lead us not into temptation, but, on the contrary, deliver us from evil." However, it must be clear that the last clause, though principally referring to the same matter, also expresses more than the first. For preservation in and from temptation leaves us, nevertheless, still in this world. It cannot be final. The Christian cannot rest content with a state in which he must be continually preserved against temptation. He wants more. He longs for perfection, for the state in which preservation against temptation will no longer be necessary. He looks forward to complete victory. It is, in final analysis, for that victory that he prays in the second part of the petition, "but deliver us from evil." With all the similarity between the two clauses, therefore, there is sufficient difference to warrant a separate discussion of the two parts of this prayer. The one part asks for preservation, the other for perfect deliverance. And in our present chapter we will limit ourselves to the first part, "Lead us not into temptation."

We are placed here face to face with the very real and very serious question of *temptation*.

Let us ask, first of all: what is meant by temptation, and what causes a temptation? The word that is translated "temptation" in the New Testament does not always have the same meaning. Sometimes it denotes trial, sometimes it means temptation. When we read in James

1:2: "My brethren, count it all joy when ye fall into diverse temptations," the word could probably better be rendered by "trials," for the text continues in verse 3: "knowing this, that the trying (or: tried character) of your faith worketh patience." The same is true of the word in verse 12: "Blessed is the man that endureth temptation: for when he is tried, he shall receive the crown of life, which the Lord hath promised to them that love him." The same word occurs in I Peter 4:12: "Beloved, think it not strange concerning the fiery trial which is to try you, as though some strange thing happened to you." And again the same word occurs in I Peter 1:6, though there it is translated by "temptations" in the King James Version, while the American Revised Version renders it, more correctly, by "trials": "Wherein ye greatly rejoice, though now for a season, if need be, ye are in heaviness through manifold temptations." On the other hand, there are several passages where the word evidently means "temptations." Thus it is clearly in James 1:13, 14: "Let no man say when he is tempted, I am tempted of God: for God cannot be tempted with evil, neither tempteth he any man: But every man is tempted, when he is drawn away of his own lust, and enticed." The word has the same meaning in Matthew 4:1, where we read: "Then was Jesus led up of the Spirit into the wilderness to be tempted of the devil." And there are other passages in Holy Writ where the word is properly translated by "tempt" or "temptation" while in some cases it is difficult to determine what is the proper rendering.

Fact is that temptation and trial are closely related concepts. They are materially the same, but they differ with respect to their aim and motive. It is, perhaps, safe to say that for the people of God all temptation is also trial, and all trial is at the same time temptation. Yet there is a good deal of difference between the two. First of all, we may note that one cannot speak of trial with respect to the wicked: for trial presupposes something good that is put to the test and that is improved by the testing process. Gold and silver are tried in order to purify them, to separate the foreign elements in them, and to enhance the beauty of their lustre. But one does not test a lump of clay or a piece of stone. So God's people are tried in as far as they are God's workmanship, created in Christ Jesus unto good works, in order that the power and beauty of the work of God's grace may become manifest, and the trial of their faith may be to "praise and honor and glory at the appearing of Jesus Christ." (I Peter 1:7) But the wicked cannot be tried, for the simple reason that there is no good in them. They are tempted: for while trial aims at the bringing to light of the beauty of the work of God's grace, temptation appeals to the sinful nature. However, it will be evident that the very same means whereby the people of God are tried also constitute for them temptations. What is a trial of their faith is at the same time a temptation for their sinful nature. When, for instance, a believer is threatened with the loss of a profitable position in the world unless he in some way becomes unfaithful and denies his Lord, his faith is being tried. But the same situation is an appeal to his sinful nature to deny Christ and keep his position. It certainly was a fiery trial of their faith when in the early church believers were sometimes confronted with the choice of confessing that Caesar was Lord or being thrown into a pot filled with boiling oil. But again, this horrible alternative also was a temptation for their flesh to bow the knee to Caesar and to deny the sole Lordship of Christ.

But there is more difference between trial and temptation. Trial always presents the truth; temptation is always a lie. Temptation always presents the way of sin and iniquity, of backsliding and unfaithfulness, of denying Christ and violating the covenant of God as something desirable, as a good that is worth striving for, in fact, as preferable to the way of obedience, righteousness, holiness, and faithfulness to Christ. When God places the tree of the knowledge of good and evil in Paradise and gives man the so-called probationary command, He proves, He tries Adam. But He tells him the truth: "the day that thou eatest thereof, thou shalt surely die." Thus it always is. It is never a good, a thing to be desired, to walk in the way of iniquity, to pursue after evil, to violate the Word of God and serve Mammon. But when the devil tempts man in paradise, he presents the lie to him: "Ye shall not surely die; ye shall be like God." And thus all temptation makes use of the lie that there is a good apart from God, in the way of sin. Temptation is moral, ethical deception. Trial deals with the truth.

Moreover, there is a fundamental difference in motive and purpose between trial and temptation. Hatred of God, hatred of one another, hatred of that which is good and delight in sin and corruption — these are the motives of all temptation. The purpose of the tempter is always God's dishonor and your destruction. It makes no difference who it is that assumes the role of tempter in regard to you. It may be your husband or wife, your brother or sister, your dearest friend; in the capacity of tempter he hates God and you and seeks your destruction. When your best friend tempts you to depart from the way of truth and righteousness and to follow after the lie and vanity, he is your enemy; and you should not hesitate to say to him, "Get thee behind me, Satan!" But trial is motivated by love, aims at the showing forth of the beauty of God's work of grace, and purposes your salvation. Temptation, then, is that lying appeal to our sinful nature that is motivated by enmity against God, His cause and His people, and aims at God's dishonor and our destruction.

Now the Lord teaches us to pray, "Lead us not into temptation."

It should be evident at once that this does not mean the same as "Grant that we may never be tempted or tried." The meaning of these words cannot be: "Lead us not into circumstances and situations that constitute temptations." That would be quite impossible. That would be equivalent to praying that the Lord might remove us from the world. As long as we are in this world we are surrounded by temptations. The three factors, or agencies, which work together to bring us into temptation are always present: for they are the well-known triumvirate of the devil, the world, and our own sinful flesh. The devil always goes about as a roaring lion, seeking whom he may devour; and, besides, there is a host of spiritual wickedness in high places against which we have our battle. In the world there is the lust of the flesh, the lust of the eyes, and the pride of life. And in a thousand ways that world, in the midst of which we have our life and walk, tempts us to leave the way of righteousness and to follow after the lusts of the flesh. Sometimes it attacks us by its vain philosophy, trying to toss us to and fro by every wind of doctrine. Then again, it tries to entice us by its pleasures and treasures, offering them to us if we will only forsake the way of truth and become unfaithful to our Lord. Or it threatens us with the fury of its wrath, deprives us of name and position in the world, mocks and blasphemes, or even erects scaffold and stake to terrorize us into denial of the name of God and our Lord Jesus Christ. And then there is the foe within the gate, our own flesh, always inclined to seek the things that are below and to listen to the siren's song of temptation. How impossible, then, that we should ever escape temptation as long as we are in this world! When you awake in the morning, you are in the midst of temptations. When you walk the street or ride the bus to your place of work, you meet with temptations everywhere. When you sit down in the evening to read your paper, temptations meet your eye. When you close your eyes in sleep, temptations remain with you in the silent watches of the night.

Nor is it the will of God that we should make the attempt to escape temptations and to withdraw ourselves from the world. Men have tried it, and failed. Men have sought the seclusion of the monastic cell, or the solitude of a lone pillar in the desert for their dwelling place; but the temptations often were multiplied. But even apart from the impossibility of such an escape from temptations, it is the will of God that His people should be right in the midst of the world, and that they should fight the good fight of faith, that no one take their crown. Surely, then, the sixth petition cannot mean: Give that we may never meet with temptations.

Nor do we do justice to the positive and definite form of this prayer when we interpret it as if it meant nothing more than that God may preserve us in the midst of temptations. To be sure, this is implied. We know that we must meet with temptations. We realize that we can never escape the evil triumvirate of the devil, the world, and our own flesh. We are conscious, too, of our own weakness. We cannot possibly stand and gain the victory in our own strength. Before we are even aware of it, the evil desires arise in our soul, the sinful thought occupies our mind. And we feel that we are in constant need of God's preserving grace if we are to stand in this bitter fight. And so we turn to the God of our salvation in Christ, the same God Who called us out of darkness into His marvelous light, and pray: "Our Father Who art in heaven,

hold Thou my hand; give Thou me grace; uphold Thou me by Thy almighty power; give Thou me light and understanding that I may always
know Thy way; and always sanctify my heart by Thy Spirit, in order
that I may not suffer defeat, but have the victory in the midst of my
enemies."

Yet a glance at the prayer as the Lord taught us to utter it must convince us that the conception here is far more positive and bold: "Lead
us not into temptation!" This surely is an acknowledgement of the
absolute sovereignty of God even in respect to sin and evil, even over
the devil, the world, and our own sinful flesh, so that we cannot be
overcome by temptation unless God Himself leads us into it. Temptation is considered as a snare into which we are led. And, to be sure, into
this snare of temptation we are led by the devil, by the world, by the
lust of our own sinful heart. But the child of God, praying from the
depths of his regenerated heart, knows that above them all, and that,
too, as their absolute Lord, stands his Father in heaven, Who employs
the devil, the world, and even his own sinful flesh for His adorable,
sovereign purpose. He knows that in the ultimate sense of the word he
can never fall into sin and thus be ensnared in the temptation, unless
God, the only Potentate of potentates, leads him into it. And deeply
aware of all this, he prays not, "Grant that I may never meet with
temptation"; nor, "In the midst of temptations preserve me"; but
positively, "Lead me not into temptation."

There arise two or three questions here which must briefly be
answered as far as this is possible. The first is whether we do not make
God the author of sin by thus presenting the matter. Our answer is:
God forbid! For "God cannot be tempted with sin, neither tempteth
He any man." He has no delight in sin, but hates it. Even when He leads
us into temptation, it is our own sinful flesh that deceives us and that
has delight in iniquity. Yet the Bible teaches us plainly that it is He
Who leads His people even when they stumble and fall. Did you never
read in the Scriptures that God, in His anger against Israel, moved
David to number the people? (II Samuel 24:1) And do not God's
people in Isaiah pray: "O Lord, why hast thou made us to err from thy
ways, and hardened our heart from thy fear?" (Isaiah 63:17) And what

else could be the meaning of this sixth petition, "Lead us not into temptation," than that God alone ultimately has the power to ensnare us in our own sinful lusts? And what else is necessary for Him to do, in order to lead us into the trap of sin, than to control and arrange for all the circumstances of the temptation, cause us to meet them, and then withhold His grace from us for a season, or even to move our own sinful flesh. Not He, but we ourselves are the author of our own sin, even when He so leads us that we fall into sin through the temptation.

The second question is: but why should the Lord ever so lead His people that they stumble and fall? There may be several reasons, but a very common one is that He desires to teach us a lesson, that we may be cured of our own conceit. Perhaps we have a deeply rooted personal weakness or sin of character; and God lets us go all the way of that sin, in order that we may learn to abhor it. Perhaps we are proud, and God causes us to stumble over our own pride, that we may be humbled. Perhaps we are forever walking on the very edge of the "world," and God lets us slip right into the world, that we may be sanctified. Perhaps we are playing with the fire of worldly pleasures; and God causes us to burn ourselves badly, that we may learn to keep our garments clean. The apostle Peter was inclined to trust in self, and to boast in his own strength. The Lord warned him. But the more he was warned, the more loudly he boasted that he was ready to go with Jesus into prison and into death, and that he would never be offended. And God prepared all the circumstances for Peter's temptation. He let him climb the full height of his self-confidence, in order then to expose his utter lack of strength by leading him into the trap of temptation when he denied his Lord. And thus the Lord sanctifies and reforms His children in a pedagogical way, that they may be saved.

But the sincere child of God is deathly afraid of this extreme remedy. He dreads it. He hopes that it may never be necessary. And so he prays, "Lead me not into temptation." There is in this prayer, first of all, the expression of a deep abhorrence of all sin and a sincere desire to fight against it. He who utters this prayer, and then wilfully seeks the temptation, is a hypocrite. There is, in the second place, a profound sense of our own weakness and helplessness, the confession that without the constant help of the grace of God we must needs perish. Finally, there is the confidence in that all-sufficient grace of God that is able to uphold us in the fight even unto the end, when we shall have the perfect victory. Watch, then, and pray! The spirit, indeed, is willing, but the flesh is weak! But when we are weak, then are we strong! For God perfects His strength in our weakness!

Chapter 10

DELIVER US FROM EVIL

That the words "deliver us from evil" express positively what was implied negatively in the prayer against temptation, we have already pointed out. The meaning of the entire petition is "Lead us not into the snare of temptation, but, on the contrary, deliver us from evil." We also explained that this second clause of the last petition of the Lord's Prayer reaches beyond the scope of the first part: to be delivered from evil implies more than to be preserved in the midst of temptation. The praying child of God has not fully disemburdened his heart before his Father in heaven, as far as his relation to the dominion and power of sin is concerned, by the prayer for preservation against the temptations that encompass him on all sides in this world. Preservation can only be a temporary measure. It cannot be final. The shipwrecked sailor certainly appreciates the life preserver or raft to which he clings on the storm-tossed ocean because it saves his life for the time being; yet to him that life belt or raft can never be more than a temporary means to keep him from drowning, and constantly he is on the lookout for a ship or cruiser that will bring him to a safe harbor. The soldier realizes that he must be fully equipped for defensive and offensive warfare; yet he looks forward to the time that he can put down his entire armor because the battle is won. So the militant Christian in this world: he realizes that he travels through the enemy's country and is in need of God's grace to preserve him in the midst of temptations; nevertheless, he longs for the day that his enemies shall be no more, the day of complete salvation and perfect victory. Hence, looking forward in hope to that final state, he prays, "Deliver us from evil."

There is a question as to the proper rendering of the original prayer.

97

Should we read "deliver us from evil" or "deliver us from the evil one"?
Our King James Version prefers the former, and so do the Latin, Ger-
man, and French translations. However, the Dutch translation reads:
"verlos ons van den Boze." And the American Revised Version also
renders the original: "deliver us from the evil one." Again, if we adopt
the rendering "deliver us from evil," is the reference only to moral evil,
to sin and corruption, or is physical evil, suffering and death, also included? As far as the form of the original word for "evil" in this prayer
is concerned, it may be translated either by "the evil one" or by "evil."
But if we consult other passages of Holy Writ where the same word
occurs, it must be admitted that the rendering, "deliver us from the evil
one" appears to deserve the preference. This is evidently the meaning of
the word in Matthew 5:37: "But let your communication be, Yea, yea;
Nay, nay: for whatsoever is more than these cometh from the evil one."
It certainly is the meaning in Matthew 13:19, where the same word is
used in the original as in our prayer: "When anyone heareth the word
of the kingdom, and understandeth it not, then cometh the wicked one,
and catcheth away that which is sown in his heart." And the same is
true in verse 38 of the same chapter: "The field is the world; the good
seed are the children of the kingdom; but the tares are the children of
the wicked one." The words of Jesus' sacerdotal prayer in John 17:15
should be translated in the same way: "I pray not that thou shouldest
take them out of the world, but that thou shouldest keep them from
the evil one." Also in Ephesians 6:16, II Thessalonians 3:3, I John
2:13, and 3:12 the same word occurs with reference to the devil. Then,
too, the close relation between this prayer and the petition against
temptation, together with the consideration that the devil is the great
tempter from the beginning, may point in the same direction. We take
it, therefore, that the proper translation is "Deliver us from the evil
one."

However, this does not limit the prayer, but rather makes it more
comprehensive. While asking for deliverance from the devil and his
power, and therefore mindful of the fact that the sinner is a slave of the
evil one, the believing Christian in this prayer is nevertheless taught to
pray for deliverance from the power of all evil. For only by being

sanctified himself and by being cleansed from all the pollution of sin is the child of God set free from the dominion of Satan. And although this refers emphatically to liberation from sin, from moral, ethical corruption, yet it should be evident that this does not exclude, but rather includes evil of every kind, also suffering and sorrow and death: for the latter are surely the wages of sin. In its comprehensive sense, therefore, the prayer looks forward to the state of final perfection in the new heavens and the new earth, where there will be no night, and God shall wipe away all tears from our eyes.

There are those who profess to be Christians, but who appear to have very little, if any, use for this petition. For, to be sure, he that utters this prayer confesses that he is not yet completely delivered from the dominion of the devil and from the power of his evil nature. And these people claim, therefore, that the believing, redeemed, regenerated, sanctified Christian cannot properly take this prayer upon his own lips. This may be a very suitable prayer for the unconverted, who is not under grace but under sin, but not for the believer. The Christian certainly must pray for constant grace of God to fight the battle against the devil and all sin: he realizes that he cannot stand without the grace of his Father in heaven. But to pray for deliverance from the dominion and power of the devil and of sin would be a denial of the work of grace accomplished in Christ Jesus and applied to him by the Holy Spirit. The believer, they emphasize, is already delivered from evil. That is the clear teaching of Holy Writ. "For sin shall not have dominion over you: for ye are not under the law, but under grace." (Romans 6:14) "But God be thanked that ye were the servants of sin, but ye have obeyed from the heart that form of doctrine that was delivered you. Being then made free from sin, ye became the servants of righteousness." (Romans 6:17, 18) "Therefore if any be in Christ, he is a new creature: old things are passed away; behold, all things are become new." (II Corinthians 5:17) "For we are his workmanship, created in Christ Jesus unto good works, which God hath before ordained that we should walk in them." (Ephesians 2:10) The believer is born of God, and "Whosoever is born of God doth not commit sin; for his seed remaineth in him; and he cannot sin, because he is born of

God." (I John 3:9) And he must reckon himself "to be dead indeed unto sin, but alive unto God through Jesus Christ our Lord." (Romans 6:11) And we are admonished: "Let not sin therefore reign in your mortal body, that ye should obey it in the lust thereof. Neither yield your members as instruments of unrighteousness unto sin; but yield yourselves unto God, as those that are alive from the dead, and your members as instruments of righteousness unto God." (Romans 6:12, 13) How then is it possible for that Christian, who is thus delivered from all the dominion of sin and of the devil, to pray, "Deliver us from evil"?

In reply to these claims of so-called perfectionism, we may begin by emphasizing all that has been said concerning the newness and perfection of the believer in Christ Jesus. And I may add immediately that no one but a new creature could possibly utter the cry, "Deliver us from evil." For the natural man is dead in trespasses and sins. He is not free. He is enslaved to sin. Sin has dominion over him. And this dominion of sin does not signify that the sinner is outwardly shackled, compelled to sin against his will and against the desires of his inmost heart, but that he is bound from within. His heart is corrupt, his will is perverse, his mind is darkened, so that he can neither truly discern nor will that which is good. He is motivated by enmity against the living God. For "the carnal mind is enmity against God: for it is not subject to the law of God, neither indeed can be." (Romans 8:7) He agrees with sin. He loves darkness rather than light. How then could such a man even begin to long and to cry for deliverance from evil? Oh, the wages which sin pays even in this life may sometimes be too bitter for him, so that he could long for deliverance from certain sinful habits in order to escape their bitter consequences. But sin as such, sin as it is transgression of the law, he cannot possibly hate; nor does he feel the dominion of sin as a yoke from which he would fain be delivered. The prayer "Deliver us from evil," therefore, is the cry that is pressed from the regenerated heart. Yes, indeed, the believer in Christ is a new creature. He is born of God. He is regenerated. And this does not mean merely that he has reformed himself, that he has been cured from some bad habits, so that he used to be a drunkard, but drinks no more, or he used to commit adultery, but now leads a clean life, or he used to swear, but now utters no more profanity. But it means that his inmost heart has been radically changed. In his inmost heart, whence are the issues of life, he has received a new life, the resurrection life of our Lord Jesus Christ. And in that inmost heart Christ, through His Spirit, has taken up His abode, and will never, even for a moment, leave it again. The Christian, therefore, is no longer a slave of sin. He is free from the dominion of the evil one. He is changed from death to life, from darkness to light. Old things have passed away; behold, all things are become new!

But does this mean that the believer, regenerated and called out of darkness into light, is completely perfected, so that there is no sin left in him whatsoever?

There is perhaps no one who, in the face of the testimony of Scripture to the contrary and in the face of reality and everyday experience, would dare to make such a claim. Oh, indeed, the Word of God teaches us that he that is born of God cannot sin, which means that exactly in as far as he is born of God, or in the capacity of one that is born of God, he cannot sin. But the same Scriptures testify but too clearly that this does not imply that the believer as he is in this world is completely free from all the pollution of sin. "If we say that we have no sin, we deceive ourselves, and the truth is not in us." (I John 1:8) And "if we say that we have not sinned, we make him a liar, and his word is not in us." (I John 1:10) And again: "For the flesh lusteth against the Spirit, and the Spirit against the flesh: and these are contrary the one to the other: so that ye cannot do the things that ye would." (Galatians 5:17) The apostle Paul gives us an inspired picture of his own experience in Romans 7:15 ff., and it is quite impossible to apply this to his state before he was converted: "For that which I do I allow not: what I would, that do I not; but what I hate, that do I. If then I do that which I would not, I consent unto the law that it is good. Now then it is no more I that do it, but sin that dwelleth in me. For I know that in me (that is, in my flesh,) dwelleth no good thing: for to will is present with me; but how to perform that which is good I find not. For the good that I would I do not: but the evil which I would not, that I do. Now if I do that I would not, it is no more I that do it, but sin that dwelleth

in me. I find then a law, that, when I would do good, evil is present
with me. For I delight in the law of God after the inward man: But I
see another law in my members, warring against the law of my mind,
and bringing me into captivity to the law of sin which is in my members. O wretched man that I am! who shall deliver me from the body of
this death?" Such is the testimony of Holy Writ. And such is the daily
experience of every Christian that takes the trouble to examine himself
before the face of God. He has a new heart, and in that inmost heart of
his he is united with Christ. But he has an old nature; and in that old
nature there are the old ruts of sin, the old motions of the lusts of the
flesh, and the lust of the eyes, and the pride of life. And his life is a
continual battle. Always again he must hear the truth as it is in Jesus to
"put off concerning the former conversation the old man, which is
corrupt according to the deceitful lusts, and be renewed in the spirit of
(your) his mind." The Christian in this world has a small beginning, a
principle, of the new obedience; but there is still the old flesh that
hankers after sin.

But perhaps you remark that in the way of watching and praying,
and of constant battle, the believer can overcome and gain the perfect
victory over sin in this life, so that he reaches a state in which he sins
no more. Or you reason that the Spirit does not only regenerate God's
elect, but also sanctifies them, and that in the process of sanctification
the believer gradually is delivered from his old nature and reaches perfection. But neither of these two views is correct. As to the latter,
sanctification consists so little of a gradual regeneration of our whole
nature, body and soul, that, on the contrary, in the way of and through
the work of sanctification the Christian is not delivered from his old,
carnal nature whatsoever, not even in the smallest degree. He always has
but a small beginning of the new obedience, no matter how old he becomes, or how truly he is sanctified. Sanctification simply does not
consist in a gradual shedding of our old nature. That old, sinful nature
goes with us to the grave. Only in and through death are we delivered
from the body of this death, not before. By sanctification we do grow
in the knowledge and grace of our Lord Jesus Christ, are strengthened
in our faith, become more fervent in love, are confirmed in hope,

receive more light and understanding of the perfect way, more strength to fight the battle and to subject the body of this death to the service of righteousness. But the old nature with its carnal lusts remains until we breathe our last. And it is exactly those Christians who are spiritually most sensitive and who have advanced farthest on the way of sanctification who will most deeply bemoan their imperfect state and confess that they have but a small beginning of the new obedience.

As to the former statement, that we, even with our sinful nature always present, can so fight and watch and pray that it is possible to live sinlessly, one has but to take sin seriously, and then cast a look into his own inner life, to know how thoroughly untrue such a statement is. I have heard the claim made occasionally that one has lived a day, a week, a month, a year, perhaps, without committing sin. But a claim of that kind is based on a very superficial notion of sin, and is the result of a very cursory examination of one's self. Oh, perhaps, we are in a position to make such a claim if we mean that for a day or week or even a longer period we never were angry or spoke a profane word, or flew into a rage, or cursed and swore, or stole or committed adultery. But how about the true, positive standard that all things must be done to the glory of God and must be motivated by the pure love of God if they are not to fall into the category of sin? Would anyone have the courage to claim that every word he spoke and every deed he did were perfect according to that standard? Or let us turn from the audible word that passed our lips and from the external deed that was performed to the secret recesses of our inner life, to our thoughts, our desires, our emotions, our motives, our hidden inclinations. Who is there that calls himself Christian and that takes things seriously, that lives at all consciously before the face of God, who would dare to claim that all his thoughts were of God, that all his desires were pure, that all his emotions were motivated by the love of God and of the brother, that never a sinful inclination arose from the dark recesses of his hidden life for a week, a day, an hour? I emphatically deny that there is a man on earth, or that there ever was or will be, outside of our Lord Jesus Christ, who could honestly step forward and say, "I am that man!" And I deny that there is any serious-minded Christian who will ever lay claim to a sinless day in this world. On the contrary, he will confess that all he does, that even the very best of his works, are defiled with sin, and that with none of them would he dare to appear in judgment before God.

It is that Christian, who is perfect in principle, but very imperfect in the body of this death, who, looking at the sinful nature that is always with him and that makes it impossible for him ever to perform anything that is not defiled with sin, cries from the depths of his regenerated heart: "Our Father who art in heaven, deliver us from the evil one, and from all evil!"

But, you say, is this prayer for deliverance, then, merely an expression of longing for the perfection of heaven, and does it not at all apply to our present life? Does not God hear this prayer even now, while we are in this world?

I reply that even if this were the case, and if there were no answer to this prayer except after death, the believer would still have to utter this cry for deliverance every day of his life. But, thanks be to God, this is not the case. Our Father in heaven hears this prayer even now, while we are still in the body of this death. And when He does hear this prayer, the first fruit is that we increase in that grace whereby we may cast an even deeper glance into the inner recesses of our existence and may discover more sins and more corruptions in our sinful nature. Sins we never noticed before then come to stand clearly before our consciousness. It results, too, in our growing more sensitive, so that we begin to consider sinful what we formerly approved, and we begin spontaneously to approve that which is excellent. The answer to this prayer further reveals itself in this, that we become more deeply sorry for our sin and our sinful condition, bemoan them in sackcloth and ashes before our God, and more earnestly seek and find the blessedness of His forgiving grace. Still more, in answer to this prayer God gives us grace to fight the battle against sin. He gives us the knowledge of "that good, and acceptable, and perfect will of God," and instills into our hearts a deeper and greater love of that perfect will. He causes us to watch and pray, and gives us more abundant grace to put off the old man and his deeds, and to put on the new man, as the elect of God: "bowels of mercies, kindness, humbleness of mind, meekness, longsuffering," and "charity, which is the bond of perfectness." (Colossians 3:12, 14) In short, He gives us grace to put on the whole armor of God, that we may fight the good fight of faith, and that in this fight we may not be defeated and overcome, but persevere even unto the end, that no one take our crown. And thus being replenished by His grace daily, we continue to pray and, indeed, cry more fervently as our prayer is heard: "Our Father who art in heaven, deliver us from evil."

O miserable man that I am! Who shall deliver me from the body of this death? I thank God through Jesus Christ our Lord! Yes, indeed, He will deliver us even unto the utmost, but not until death comes to open the door for us into the heavenly perfection. Ultimately this prayer is heard when the earthly house of this tabernacle is dissolved, and we enter into the house of God not made with hands, eternal in the heavens. Yea, final perfection and deliverance from the evil one, and from all evil, does not come until the day of the Lord, when He shall raise our corruptible and mortal bodies into the glory of incorruptibility and immortality, and give us our place forever in the heavenly tabernacle of God. In last analysis it is to that perfection that this prayer looks forward; and it is with his eye on that glorious state of perfect righteousness that the believer utters this prayer, "Deliver us from the evil one."

This, then, is the spiritual disposition required to utter this final petition of the Lord's Prayer in spirit and in truth: a deep and earnest longing for complete perfection. It implies a deep and growing spiritual knowledge of our sinful condition, a profound consciousness of sin. It presupposes a deeply rooted hatred and abhorrence of sin, of all sin, and that, too, because sin is contrary to the will of God. It presupposes that he who utters this prayer is moved by a strong resolution to fight against all evil and to keep all the commandments of God. For how shall one bring this prayer before the face of the Holy One as long as there is even one sin which he nourishes and presses to his bosom? There is, moreover, in this prayer the expression of a deep consciousness of our utter dependence upon the grace of God and of the truth of the words of Jesus, "Without me ye can do nothing." As long as we imagine that in any sense we can deliver ourselves from evil, this prayer has no room in our hearts. And so this last petition is motivated by the love of the bride for the bridegroom and by the desire to be like Him at His coming.

Yea, come, Lord Jesus!

Chapter 11

THE DOXOLOGY

"For thine is the kingdom, and the power, and the glory, for ever. Amen." These words constitute the doxology of the Lord's Prayer as it has been adopted and used by the church from earliest times. If you consult the American Revised Version of the Bible, however, you will discover that these words are omitted. This omission means that it is now quite generally accepted, on the basis of textual criticism, that the doxology does not belong to the text of the Lord's Prayer as originally given by our Savior to His disciples, and that it was inserted later.

I cannot enter into this critical question here. All I wish to say now is that, even though it must be admitted that the preponderance of the original manuscripts of the New Testament is in favor of its omission from the text in Matthew, it is safe to assume that the church will always continue to close the Lord's Prayer with this doxology. And there is good reason not only for the continuance of this custom, but also for considering these closing words as quite Scriptural and, therefore, for treating it in our discussion as a genuine part of the Lord's Prayer. Not only does this prayer without the doxology come to an unnaturally abrupt close, but doxologies of this kind abound in Scripture, so that the closing words of the model prayer may certainly be said to be inspired as to their contents. The apostle Paul writes at the close of his eleventh chapter of the Epistle to the Romans: "For of him, and through him and to him, are all things: to whom be glory for ever. Amen." And at the close of the entire epistle he writes: "To God, only wise, be glory through Jesus Christ for ever. Amen." (Romans 16:27) In Philippians 4:20 we read: "Now unto God and our Father be glory for ever and ever. Amen." In his introduction to the Book of Revelation,

John writes: "Unto him that loved us, and washed us from our sins in his own blood, . . .to him be glory and dominion for ever and ever. Amen." (Revelation 1:5, 6) The four and twenty elders fall down to worship Him that sitteth upon the throne, saying: "Thou art worthy, O Lord, to receive glory and honour and power: for thou hast created all things, and for thy pleasure they are and were created." (Revelation 4:11) And all creation breaks forth in praise unto God and the Lamb in these words: "Blessing, and honour, and glory, and power, be unto him that sitteth upon the throne, and unto the Lamb for ever and ever." (Revelation 5:13) And the holy angels respond to the praise of the redeemed church in glory, "Saying, Amen: Blessing, and glory, and wisdom, and thanksgiving, and honour, and power, and might, be unto our God for ever and ever. Amen." (Revelation 7:12) It seems to me, therefore, that the Lord Jesus never intended us to close our prayers abruptly with the word "evil," and that, textual criticism notwithstanding, the Revised Version had served us better by leaving this beautiful doxology in the body of the text.

Let us first try to understand the meaning of these closing words, in order then to inquire into their significance in relation to the whole of this perfect prayer. As we have stated, these words are a doxology, or ascription of praise to God. In this doxology we ascribe to God three things: the kingdom, the power, and the glory. It will be evident that the words "for ever" are meant to modify all three, so that the meaning is: Thine is the kingdom forever; Thine is the power forever; and Thine is the glory forever. The whole doxology, as well as the whole of our prayer, is closed with the solemn assurance of faith and confidence: Amen.

Thine is the kingdom for ever! In this part of the doxology the child of God ascribes to his Father in heaven absolute sovereignty over all things, undisputed and for ever. This means, first of all, that God has the sole authority, the exclusive prerogative to rule, not only over His kingdom as it is established in Jesus Christ our Lord, but over all things and all creatures, in the whole universe. He is Lord. But these words also declare that God actually has the dominion, that He always does rule with sovereign might, and that no one is ever able to deprive Him of the reins of government. Two things, therefore, are expressed here: "Thou, O our Father in heaven, art the only rightful Sovereign over all things, and must be acknowledged as such"; and: "Thou, O Lord of heaven and earth, dost actually govern all things, so that nothing ever betides in all the wide creation without Thy sovereign will." And do not overlook the fact that the exclusiveness of this dominion of the Most High is emphasized in this doxology. We are taught here not to ascribe dominion, some dominion, perhaps the highest authority and sovereignty, to God; but absolutely all authority and dominion is ascribed to God alone. For we are instructed to say, "Thine is *the* kingdom." God is not *a* sovereign, while there are other sovereigns beside Him, or perhaps under Him; but He is *the* Lord, the sole Sovereign, the only Potentate of potentates in heaven and on earth. He alone is the authority; His alone is the power to rule. There is absolutely nothing excluded from this kingdom of God. He always rules alone: for He is God, and there is none beside Him.

That is a bold statement to make in this world of sin and corruption in which the powers of darkness always appear to dispute the sovereignty of God, and often seem to have considerable success in their attempt to rebel against the Most High. Perhaps it would be easier for some to take this doxology upon their lips if they might change its tense into the future and say, "Thine will be the kingdom when all things shall be finished." For many people it would seem rather difficult to believe that God always has the dominion. They have a rather dualistic conception of things. The devil and all the powers of darkness, so they think, do also have dominion, and for a time, at least, they successfully opposed the kingdom of God. Their consolation is, however, that God's dominion is more powerful and more efficient than the kingdom of darkness, and that in the end God will overcome them all. They look upon the relation between the Most High and the devil as similar to that of an earthly sovereign over against a hostile invader and pretender to the throne, who is temporarily successful, but who will ultimately be expelled by the king who will then hold undisputed sway in his domain. But we may not thus think of our Father in heaven. His is *the* kingdom. And notice that we should add here:

forever! This modifier does not merely look to the future, when all the powers of darkness shall be destroyed. It has reference to the present and to all the past as well. God always did rule; He always does rule; and He always will rule as the sole and absolute Sovereign over all things. Even when the devil and all the powers of darkness *appear* to rule, God rules. Even when they think they rule, as in the vain imagination of their foolish minds they no doubt do, God rules. He has no battle to maintain His rule; He *rules*. He does not defend His dominion; He *has* dominion. God is *the* Lord forever! That is what the believer who understands something of the sovereignty of his Father in heaven means when he says: "Thine is the kingdom!"

The same exclusiveness must be emphasized in our explanation of the second element of the doxology: Thine is the power for ever! The word that is used here in the original for "power" signifies inherent force or energy to accomplish something. There is another word for power in Scripture, the word that is used, for instance, by our Savior when He says, "Unto me is given all power in heaven and on earth," and which emphasizes the notion of authority. The term that is used here in the doxology, however, is the word from which our English word "dynamic" is derived. It denotes ability to do things. This is here ascribed to God. His is the power to accomplish whatsoever He wills. There is no limit to this power of God. Only His own Being or nature determines what He is able to do. For notice that also here the ascription of praise to the Most High is exclusive and absolute: "Thine is *the* power." This is not the same as saying that God is very powerful, or that He is more powerful than any other being, or even that He is supremely powerful. It means that He is all-powerful, for the simple reason that all power is strictly His. Not only the power that is within God is His, but also the force and ability of the creature is His; and without Him there is no power anywhere in all this wide creation. The power of the golden sunlight and of the gentle rain, the power that reveals itself in the sprouting grass and in the blooming flowers, the force of the flashing lightning and of the roaring thunder and of the howling tempest; the explosive power of the bombs that are dropped by the airforces of the warring nations; the energy of the living creature, of man and beast, of angels and demons, their power to think, to will, to speak and to act, to sing or to lament, to praise or to curse, to do good or evil — all power is of God. There is no creature in heaven, on earth, or in the abyss that has power in itself; it is all of Him Who created all things and Who constantly upholds them by the Word of His power. This is what the church expresses in this part of the doxology, "Thine is *the* power."

And this is true *for ever*. It will not *become* thus in some future age, when all power of opposition and resistance to God's power shall have been overcome. There never was, there is not now, and there never will be any power independent of God that is able to resist the power of God. Even though the devil and all the wicked in their vain imagination and unspeakable folly purpose in their heart an attempt to oppose the Most High, and even though they may seem often to be successful in their designs to frustrate the work of God, the day of the theodicy will reveal clearly that they could execute only the good pleasure of the Almighty. For His is the power for ever!

But if all the dominion and authority and power and might is of God, it follows that His also is all the glory: Thine is the glory for ever! To ascribe glory to God is to say that He is good, that He is infinitely good, that He is the implication of all infinite perfections, of truth and faithfulness, of knowledge and wisdom, of power and might, of holiness and righteousness, of grace and beauty, of love and life; and this infinite goodness of God shines forth, is displayed before our eyes. In all the works of God's hands His glory shines forth. In this connection it must also be emphasized that there is no glory anywhere that is not of God. There is a glory of the sun, and a glory of the moon, and a glory of the stars; there is a glory of the heavens and a glory of the earth; there is a glory of the woods and of the mountains, of the rivers and of the oceans; there is a glory of the beasts of the field and of the cattle on a thousand hills; there is a glory of man and a glory of angels. But never is the glory of the creature to be acknowledged: for it is all the radiation of the infinite goodness of God. And the church beholds His glory above all in the face of Jesus Christ, Who was delivered for our transgressions, and raised for our justification, and

Whom God hath exalted at His right hand, far above all powers and principalities, and every name that is named, and through Whom the marvelous power and unsearchable wisdom, the unfathomable love and abundant mercy, the absolute holiness and unchangeable righteousness, the beauty of His grace and the blessedness of His life are revealed. Conscious of all this, the church prostrates herself in worship and adoration, and concludes her prayers with this beautiful ascription of praise: "Thine is the kingdom, and the power, and the glory, for ever!"

But let us now consider this doxology from the viewpoint of its significance in relation to our prayer. The question arises, first of all: what spiritual disposition of our heart and mind is required in order to utter this doxology in spirit and in truth? If my prayer is to be more than the mechanical saying of my "paternosters," or the moving of a bead, if there is to be harmony between the work of my lips and the inner state of my heart when I utter this ascription of praise to God, what must be my spiritual disposition or attitude?

The answer is briefly: that of worship. And worship means that I have really been in the sanctuary, that I have felt myself in the presence of God, that I have received a glimpse of His infinite glory and beauty of holiness, and that, realizing my own nothingness in His glorious presence, I prostrate myself before Him and say, "O, my God!" I said that we received a *glimpse* of His infinite glory: for more may not be said as long as we are in "the body of this death." We do not yet really stand in the presence of God in all its implications. And a good thing it is that we do not. Those who ever did were almost consumed by the glory of His holiness. Even the seraphim cover their faces in His presence. Isaiah, seeing Him in a vision, could only cry out, "Woe is me, I am undone!" When the glory of Christ's divinity flashed through His humanity, Peter cried out, "Lord, depart from me, for I am a sinful man!" And we would do the same thing if, in our present state, we would really be brought face to face with the infinitely glorious God. But that is now impossible. When we ourselves are changed, made like unto our glorious Lord, we may see Him face to face: for then we shall be like Him. Now we see as in a glass darkly, even when we pray. We obtain a glimpse of His glory. We behold the reflection of His glorious majesty through His Word. Through His Spirit we have the knowledge of Him, not only in our heads but in our hearts. But this glimpse is sufficient to fill our soul with holy awe in His presence. And if thus we come before the living God in the face of Jesus Christ our Lord, and are really impressed by His infinite goodness and glorious majesty, we realize that we can do only one thing: worship! And, O, what marvelous power of grace it is whereby the rebellious and cursing sinner is so changed that he prostrates himself in humble adoration before the throne of the Most High and cries out: "Our Father, who art in heaven, Thine is the kingdom, and the power, and the glory, for ever!"

But there is more. This doxology also stands in a very definite relation to our whole prayer as expressed in the several petitions of this perfect model. For let us not overlook that the little but significant conjunction *for* connects this doxology with the whole prayer: "*For* thine is the kingdom, and the power, and the glory, for ever." This signifies that in this doxology I express a reason for my prayer, a ground for all my petitions. How true this is and how cogent a reason and how firm a ground for my prayer there is in this closing ascription of praise to God is especially evident as soon as we connect the doxology with the address, as, of course, should be done: "For Thine, O our Father who art in heaven, is the kingdom, and the power, and the glory, for ever!" In this doxology, therefore, the child of God motivates his whole prayer. He expresses the reason here, first of all, for the fact that he prays at all, and that he prays to his Father in heaven alone. In it he declares: "Our Father, Who art highly exalted above all that is named creature, Who lovest me from before the foundation of the world, Who hast revealed Thine unfathomable love to me in the death and resurrection of Thine only begotten Son, to Thee and to Thee alone I pray, in Thee and in Thee alone do I put my confidence, from Thee and from Thee alone do I expect all good things, to Thee and to Thee alone I ascribe all honor and praise; for I know that Thou art strong to save, and willing to help and deliver me, and that Thou alone art worthy of all adoration: because Thine, O Father, is the kingdom, and the power, and glory, for ever!"

Secondly, the doxology also expresses the reason why the believer prayed as he did, why he presented before the throne of grace the petitions of this perfect prayer. What did we ask for in this prayer which the Lord taught us to pray? Negatively expressed, we did not ask for carnal things, for earthly peace and prosperity, for health and abundance; we did not attempt to impose our will upon the will of the Almighty; we did not criticize His government of the world or His direction of our personal lives; we did not make an attempt to prescribe to Him just how He should direct all things. Positively expressed, we prayed for the things that concerned the glory of His name, the coming of His kingdom, the realization of and the obedience to His will, *first of all,* and subordinated all the rest of our prayer strictly to these highest and most important matters. We prayed for bread for one day, and declared that we would not be anxious for the morrow, even though the bread basket were empty tonight. We expressed before His face that we were sorry for our sins, and that we could have no rest until He gave us the assurance of His blessed forgiveness; that we dread the temptations and earnestly implored His preserving grace; that we hate all evil and long for the day of final deliverance from all corruption. For these things we prayed and there was not a carnal desire expressed in the whole of our request. One act of worship our prayer was, and the whole concentrated around the living God and His glory. Why? What is the reason that all true prayer must needs be thus, and why does the truly praying child of God realize that no other prayer can possibly be proper and pleasing in the sight of God? The reason is expressed in the close of the prayer, this beautiful doxology: "For thine is the kingdom, and the power, and the glory, for ever!"

If we have prayed thus, then — but then only — can we close our prayers with the very significant word *Amen.* Perhaps in our daily prayers the word *Amen* means little more than that it is a sign that we have finished our petitions. But the word has a very profound meaning, and its use at the close of our prayers is very significant. By it we affix a seal to our entire prayer. By saying *amen* we really become very bold and bind the living God to give us just what we asked of Him. *Amen* is a Hebrew word. It is derived from a word that means to establish, to make firm, or to be steadfast and unmovable. Hence, the word *amen* signifies: it is true, it is established, it is absolutely sure. The Lord Jesus often employed the word to emphasize the truth and certainty of His doctrine, and then it is translated in our English Bible by "verily, verily." And Christ Himself is called "the Amen, the faithful and true witness." (Revelation 3:14) When, therefore, we use this word at the close of our prayers, we say with reference to them: it is established, it is certain and true!

Now when we thus close our prayers, we do a very serious thing. For then we declare, first of all, before the face of God that in our prayers we were true, that we did not lie when we prayed, that we did not play the hypocrite, but that we are sure that the things we prayed for are the objects of the desire of our inmost heart. We express that in the uprightness of our heart, even though it was with much imperfection, we asked for the things of God in the first place, and for our own interests only in so far as they would tend to the glory of God and the coming of His kingdom. We say that we are sure that we are quite satisfied with bread for today, and that we long for the forgiveness of sins, and for the deliverance from evil, and for final perfection. We say: "Amen; O Father, Who knowest the hearts and provest the reins, Thou knowest that my prayer was in truth and that I earnestly desire these things of Thee."

Secondly, this "amen" expressed that it is established and certain that God will hear my prayer and give me exactly that which I asked for. This must be emphasized. "Amen" does not mean that God will give me *something* though it may be the very opposite from what I asked of Him. Thus it is often explained. Many people seem to consider it very pious to say that even though God does not give us what we ask, He will surely give us some good thing. But that is not the meaning of the word *amen.* Nor is it pious. It usually means that we take no pains to pray according to the will of God, but that we ask for all kinds of carnal things. And then the Lord does not hear and give us what we ask of Him. But when we pray anything according to His will, we know that He surely hears us, and that He gives unto us all we ask of Him abundantly.

Conscious, therefore, of our weakness and imperfection, and of our inclination to pray according to the flesh rather than according to the will of God, we may well close our series of meditations on the Lord's Prayer with the petition: "Lord, so teach me to pray according to Thy will, that I may be able to say: Amen, even so, Lord, I know that Thou wilt grant all my requests." Then the peace of God which passeth all understanding shall keep our hearts and minds through Christ Jesus!